Series 6

Exam
Practice Questions

I0880206

Mometrix
TEST PREPARATION

DEAR FUTURE EXAM SUCCESS STORY

First of all, **THANK YOU** for purchasing Mometrix study materials!

Second, congratulations! You are one of the few determined test-takers who are committed to doing whatever it takes to excel on your exam. **You have come to the right place.** We developed these practice tests with one goal in mind: to deliver you the best possible approximation of the questions you will see on test day.

Standardized testing is one of the biggest obstacles on your road to success, which only increases the importance of doing well in the high-pressure, high-stakes environment of test day. Your results on this test could have a significant impact on your future, and these practice tests will give you the repetitions you need to build your familiarity and confidence with the test content and format to help you achieve your full potential on test day.

Your success is our success

We would love to hear from you! If you would like to share the story of your exam success or if you have any questions or comments in regard to our products, please contact us at **800-673-8175** or **support@mometrix.com**.

Thanks again for your business and we wish you continued success!

Sincerely,
The Mometrix Test Preparation Team

Written and edited by the Mometrix Exam Secrets Test Prep Team
Printed in the United States of America

Table of Contents

Practice Test #1

1. FINRA Rule 8312 requires which of the following Civil Judicial Disclosures to be made permanently public via the BrokerCheck system?

a. Former associates of a member who were not associated with the member for the preceding ten years, were registered on or after August 16, 1999, and were party to a civil injunction involving investment-related activities.
b. Former associates of a member who were not associated with the member for the preceding ten years and at any previous time were party to a final regulatory action.
c. Former associates of a member who were registered on or after August 16, 1999, and were party to an investment-related civil action initiated by a financial regulatory authority, state or foreign, that had been dismissed as the result of a settlement agreement.
d. All of the above

2. Which of the following FINRA rules is associated with continuing education requirements?

a. FINRA Rule 2266
b. FINRA Rule 11870
c. FINRA Rule 1250
d. FINRA 1122

3. FINRA Rule 3220 requires which of the following?

I. Members must keep separate records of all gifts or gratuities.
II. Members' gifts or gratuities made in relation to the business of the employer of the person who receives it must not exceed $250 per year.
III. An exclusion for any payments that are made related to authentic written contracts for employment.
IV. Members' gifts or gratuities made in relation to the business of the employer of the person who receives it must not exceed $100 per year.

a. I. and II.
b. I., III., and IV.
c. I., II., and III.
d. I. and IV.

4. In consideration of FINRA Rule 2111, which of the following describes a broker's suitability obligation known as "quantitative suitability"?

a. A broker who has authority and control over a customer's account must use the standard of "reasonableness" when determining whether a series of proposed securities transactions are not excessive in relation to this particular account.
b. A broker must consider the specific customer's investment profile when determining, using a "reasonableness" standard, the suitability of a security transaction or investment strategy for that customer.
c. A broker, in determining that a given security transaction or investment strategy is suitable for at least "some" investors, must exercise reasonable diligence in researching and understanding the nature of a proposed security transaction or investment strategy, and also the potential risks and rewards.
d. None of the above.

5. NASD Rule 1060(b) states that member firms may compensate non-registered foreign persons for business, and specifically transactions, directed to them by said foreign persons as long as which of the following conditions is met?

I. The customer is provided a document detailing the compensation that was paid to the finders.
II. The transaction confirmation specifies that an agreed-upon finder's fee was paid as a result of the transaction.
III. The finders are either living here and not US citizens, or are foreign entities living abroad.

a. I. and II.
b. III. only
c. I., II., and III.
d. II. and III.

6. The term "security" can be defined by which of the following characteristics?

I. May be riskless.
II. Can be easily transferred between two parties.
III. Can be traded for some value.
IV. Primarily is either equity or debt.

a. II., III., and IV.
b. I., II., and IV.
c. II. and IV.
d. I. and III.

7. Which of the following is NOT an example of a security?

a. Exchange-traded funds (ETFs)
b. Fixed annuities
c. Mutual funds
d. Variable annuities

8. The following are all considered assets as they relate to a balance sheet EXCEPT:

a. Securities
b. Property
c. Accounts payable
d. Accounts receivable

9. Stock that has been sold publicly as an investment and still currently remains with those investors, having not been repurchased by the issuing corporation, is called:

a. Treasury stock
b. Outstanding stock
c. Authorized stock
d. None of the above

10. Given the following issued and outstanding stock amounts, calculate the resulting amount of treasury stock for this corporation.

Authorized Stock:	90,000
Issued Stock:	73,000
Outstanding Stock:	51,000

a. 22,000
b. 39,000
c. 124,000
d. 17,000

11. In a rights offering, all of the following are true EXCEPT:

a. Shareholders may "exercise" their right by buying new additional shares.
b. Rights may "expire" if market conditions regarding the stock make buying new additional shares unfavorable to the shareholder.
c. The right to purchase new shares is at the stock's book value.
d. Shareholders may "sell" their rights to purchase new shares.

12. Of the following statements below, which describe rights investors possess as shareholders in a corporation?

I. Inspection of the corporation's books and records.
II. Vote regarding mergers, acquisitions, and stock splits.
III. Examination of the corporation's "confidential" financial data.
IV. Vote in the election of the board of directors.

a. I. and IV.
b. I., II., and IV.
c. I., III., and IV.
d. IV. only.

13. Which of the terms below describes the date an investor who purchased a security is officially recorded as the owner of record?

a. Settlement date
b. Payment date
c. Declaration date
d. Trade date

14. Which of the following are consequences for a customer in violation of Regulation T?

a. Securities that are the subject of the violation, and thus unpaid for, will be sold on the sixth business day after the trade date, with the customer being held responsible for any loss that may be incurred as a result of that sale.
b. Any purchases that the customer would like to make in relation to this account over the next 90 days will require money for the transaction being deposited into the account first.
c. The customer's account will be sold out and a freeze will be placed on it.
d. All of the above

15. Of the types of preferred stock, which provides its holders the right to be provided with both the preferred dividend plus any additional common stock dividends that may be distributed?

a. Cumulative preferred
b. Convertible preferred
c. Noncumulative preferred
d. Participating preferred

16. Calculate the number of common stock shares that result from the exchange of 2 percent convertible preferred stock carrying a conversion price of $10 per share.

a. 20
b. 50
c. 10
d. 2

17. Which of the following statements associated with a corporation's payment of dividends is NOT true?

a. A corporation's board of directors is responsible for deciding the payment date, or dividend distribution date to shareholders.
b. Registered representatives may utilize as the sole justification for purchase of a certain stock, an upcoming dividend payment.
c. For an investor to be eligible to receive a declared dividend, they must have become the recorded owner of the stock BEFORE the ex-dividend date.
d. Investors receiving dividends in a given year will be charged a 15 percent tax on those dividends for that year.

18. What type of security offers the holder the chance to buy common stock at a specific subscription price with the offer to do so lasting up to 10 years?

a. Warrants
b. Calls
c. Puts
d. Options

19. Which of the following describe ways that individual investors may obtain warrants?

a. Companies may offer them as an add-on to their bond offering as a way to more aggressively market to potential investors.
b. Companies may issue them to investors who purchased common stock in their initial public offering.
c. Through a secondary market.
d. All of the above

20. All of the following statements are true of options EXCEPT:

a. The option premium is the payment made by the buyer of an option contract to a seller.
b. A put option offers its buyer the right to sell a specific security for a specific price and only for a specific period of time.
c. The seller of an option contract always retains the right to decline proceeding with the transaction to buy or sell.
d. A call option offers its buyer the right to buy a specific security for a specific price and only for a specific period of time.

21. Which of the following could be TRUE of investors who have a "bullish" outlook on a security and its potential price movement?

a. Sell put options so as to benefit from the obligation to buy a security at a fixed price that is set lower than the price they believe the security will increase to.
b. Generally believe the security will be increasing in price.
c. Purchase call options so as to benefit from the opportunity to buy a security at a fixed price that is lower than the price they believe the security will increase to.
d. All of the above

22. An investor purchases a 1 PRK May 45 call for $7. What is the purchase price at which the option provides them the right to buy security PRK?

a. PRK @ $7 per share
b. PRK @ $45 per share
c. PRK @ $1 per share
d. None of the above

23. Which of the following describes the role of a firm acting as a broker?

I. Fills customer's orders by either selling from or buying for their own account.
II. Acts as an agent to execute orders.
III. Receives a commission for its services.
IV. Acts as a market maker for a security.

a. II. and III.
b. I. and IV.
c. I., II., and IV.
d. I., II., and III.

24. All of the following describe characteristics of corporate bondholders EXCEPT:

a. They come before common and preferred stockholders in the order of who will be paid if liquidation should occur.
b. They may be given the opportunity to influence corporate management if the corporation falls behind on interest and principal payments or defaults entirely.
c. They assume a level of ownership in the corporation.
d. They are not afforded voting rights as long as the corporation remains current in its debt payments.

25. Of the following, which is known to be the largest issuer of debt?

a. Municipalities
b. US Government
c. Corporations
d. None of the above

26. Which type of bond issuance involves NO actual bond certificate being issued?

a. Book entry
b. Principal-only registration
c. Bearer bonds
d. All of the above

27. Which of the following can be used interchangeably with the term "par value"?

a. Loan amount
b. Principal amount
c. Face value
d. All of the above

28. What would be the quoted price for a corporate bond listed at 98.74?

a. $9.874
b. $9,874.00
c. $987.40
d. None of the above

29. Which type of yield is fixed at the time it is issued and printed on the bond, and is known as the bond's coupon rate?

a. Yield to maturity
b. Nominal yield
c. Current yield
d. None of the above

30. For a bond investment, as the price of the bond rises, the yield will:

a. Fall
b. Stay constant
c. Be unknown, depending on other factors
d. Rise

31. Calculate the current yield of this bond listed at 105 and with a nominal yield of 7 percent.

a. 10.5 percent
b. 7.77 percent
c. 6.67 percent
d. 7 percent

32. Which of the following can be categorized as secured bonds?

I. Equipment trust certificates
II. Debentures
III. Collateral trust certificates
IV. Mortgage bonds

a. I. and III.
b. I., III., and IV.
c. I., II., and III.
d. II. and IV.

33. All of the following describe characteristics of zero coupon bonds EXCEPT:

a. Provides for payment of semiannual interest.
b. Income tax imposed on the bond's annual appreciation.
c. Issued at a price discounted from par value.
d. Price is sensitive to changes in interest rates.

34. How many shares will the holder of a convertible bond receive upon converting it into RK common stock at $5 per share?

a. 20 shares
b. 200 shares
c. 120 shares
d. 2,000 shares

35. How many shares will the holder of convertible preferred stock receive upon converting into GJ common stock at $20 per share?

a. 50 shares
b. 75 shares
c. 5 shares
d. 500 shares

36. Calculate the parity price for a convertible bond with a current market value of $1,750 and a JG common stock conversion price of $50.

a. $87.50
b. $20.00
c. $875.00
d. $35.00

37. All of the following are true of Treasury bills EXCEPT:

a. Awarded by the Treasury Department via weekly auctions.
b. Maturities range from 4 to 52 weeks.
c. Priced at a discount from par.
d. Pay semiannual interest.

38. Which of the following are categorized as nonmarketable government securities?

I. Treasury STRIPS
II. Series EE
III. Series HH
IV. Treasury receipts

a. I., II., and IV.
b. I. and IV.
c. I., II., and III.
d. II. and III.

39. Which of the following is the only agency with securities that are backed by the full faith and credit of the US government?

a. FHLMC
b. GNMA
c. FNMA
d. None of the above

40. Which of the following is a publicly traded company?

I. GNMA
II. FNMA
III. CMO
IV. FHLMC

a. I., II., and IV.
b. I. and III.
c. II. and IV.
d. II. only.

41. Of the following statements, which is TRUE of FNMA (the Federal National Mortgage Association)?

a. Purchases mortgages with the intent to bundle them as mortgage-backed securities.
b. Also known as Fannie Mac.
c. Securities created provide investors with tax-free interest income.
d. Notes created are only issued in denominations of $5,000.

42. Considering collateralized mortgage obligations (CMOs), which of the following describes the primary risk faced by investors in these securities?

a. Changes in interest rates
b. Early refinancing
c. Late interest and principal payments
d. None of the above

43. Which of the following statements are TRUE of collateralized mortgage obligations (CMOs)?

a. There is a secondary market for these securities.
b. Pools of mortgages act as collateral for these securities.
c. Rate of payment is determined by the rate of refinancing, therefore a rise in interest rates may slow refinances and accordingly repayments to investors.
d. All of the above

44. Which type of municipal bond is backed by the full faith and credit of its issuing organization and the taxes it is able to raise to repay the obligations?

a. Industrial development bonds
b. Revenue bonds
c. General obligation bonds
d. None of the above

45. Given the following information, calculate the tax equivalent yield for an investor who is contemplating whether to invest in a municipal bond or a corporate bond.

Coupon rate of municipal bond: 5 percent
Investor's tax bracket: 22 percent

a. 6.25 percent
b. 64 percent
c. 63 percent
d. 6.4 percent

46. Given that a municipal bond is purchased by investors within their state of residence, which of the following types of tax will the interest earned be subject to?

a. Local
b. Federal
c. State
d. None of the above

47. All of these can be categorized as government money market instruments EXCEPT:

a. Federal funds loans
b. Short-term discount notes
c. Treasury securities with less than one year left
d. Treasury bills

48. When considering negotiable certificates of deposit, what is the amount that the Federal Deposit Insurance Corporation (FDIC) insures up to?

a. $1,000,000
b. $500,000
c. $250,000
d. $100,000

49. Commercial paper has which of the following characteristics?

I. Maturity can range from 30 days to 10+ years
II. Unsecured promissory note
III. Issued at discount of face value
IV. Maturities range from 1 to 270 days

a. II. and III.
b. II., III., and IV.
c. II. and IV.
d. I., II., and III.

50. Given that FINRA Rule 2090 stipulates that certain questions must be asked of customers during the process of opening and servicing their account, which of the following is REQUIRED before opening an account on behalf of a customer?

a. Net worth
b. Investment objectives
c. Employment status
d. Date of birth

51. Regarding FINRA's code of procedure guidelines for member violation investigations, all of the following are true EXCEPT:

a. To begin its investigation, FINRA will notify the member of the complaint against it and request its written response within 60 days.
b. If allegations are found to be without merit, FINRA can choose to immediately dismiss without further investigation.
c. FINRA routinely performs reviews of member firms.
d. FINRA may choose to resolve an allegation through a formal hearing.

52. A minor rule violation involves which of the following?

a. The maximum punishment that can result is a censure and a $2,500 fine.
b. Upon signing and committing to the minor rule violation process, the accused member relinquishes its right to appeal whatever decision is handed down.
c. Once provided the opportunity to participate in the minor rule violation process, the member has 10 days to commit to it.
d. All of the above

53. FINRA sets forth which of the following penalties for member violations of its rules?

I. Barred for life
II. Fine not to exceed $2,500
III. Suspension for up to five years
IV. Censure

a. II., III., and IV.
b. I. and IV.
c. I., II., III., and IV.
d. I., III., and IV.

54. To what organization must an appeal of a FINRA violation decision be made?

a. National Adjudicatory Counsel (NAC)
b. Office of Supervisory Jurisdiction (OSJ)
c. Division of Enforcement (DOE)
d. FINRA

55. FINRA's code of arbitration states that:

a. Industry members be provided arbitration as one of several options for dispute resolution.
b. Broker-dealers are required to have customers sign a customer agreement upon opening an account with them.
c. It is not implied that a customer agrees to settle disputes through arbitration, but instead they must agree in writing to that sort of resolution up front.
d. The statute of limitations for arbitration is 10 years from the event in dispute.

56. In which cases can arbitration be utilized as the dispute resolution of choice?

a. Registered representative vs. a member
b. Customer vs. a member
c. Bank vs. a member
d. All of the above

57. Awards that come as the result of the arbitration process are NOT:

a. For monetary payments, required to be paid within 30 days
b. Available for appeal
c. Required to be paid under penalty of suspension
d. All of the above

58. Which type of dispute resolution concludes as an agreement, an impasse, or withdrawal from the process?

a. Simplified arbitration
b. Panel arbitration
c. Mediation
d. None of the above

59. Which of the following describes the settlement date for government bond transactions?

a. Next business day after the trade date
b. Same day as the trade date
c. Three business days after the trade date
d. None of the above

60. All of these statements are true of payment dates for trade transactions EXCEPT:

a. Payment date is five business days after trade date.
b. Defined as the date payment is due for the purchase of securities.
c. Firms have the option to require the payment date to be earlier than industry rules state.
d. The SEC regulates payment dates under the authority of Regulation T of the Securities Exchange Act of 1934.

61. A variable annuity is one of the three basic types of annuities available to investors. Which of the following are characteristics of that type of investment instrument?

I. Susceptible to the risk of inflation.
II. Representatives need only obtain an insurance license to sell these.
III. The return is guaranteed at a specific set minimum.
IV. The portfolio consists of investments that include stocks and mutual fund shares.

a. II., III., and IV.
b. I. and IV.
c. I. and II.
d. IV. only

62. Which of the following was created as an extension of the Gramm-Leach-Bliley Act?

a. Investment Advisers Act of 1940
b. Regulation S-P
c. Employee Retirement Income Security Act of 1974
d. None of the above

63. An investor is trying to choose which method of holding securities will best suit her needs. She would like to have the flexibility of reinvesting any resulting distributions while having the ability to easily transfer ownership of the securities. Which method would be most appropriate for this investor?

a. Transfer and ship
b. Transfer and hold in safekeeping
c. Hold in street name
d. None of the above

64. The Securities Investor Protection Corporation (SIPC) provides relief via industry-funded insurance in the event of the failure of a broker-dealer firm. Given the customer information below, which of these individuals would receive full cash coverage by the SIPC upon the failure of their broker-dealer firm?

I. Customer A: $487,000 in cash
II. Customer B: $253,000 in cash
III. Customer C: $127,000 in cash
IV. Customer D: $242,000 in cash

a. II., III., and IV.
b. III. and IV.
c. III. only
d. II. and IV.

65. A customer would like to participate in a joint account with his representative. Can the representative share in the profits of this account, and if so, to what degree?

a. Yes, but only if they have actually invested funds into the account.
b. Yes, but the degree to which they share in the profit will only be in proportion to the amount they have invested into the account.
c. Yes, if the firm approves of the joint account prior to it being opened.
d. All of the above

66. A registered representative has been presented with the opportunity to purchase rental property. Is it required that she receive approval from her firm prior to purchasing the property?

a. No, it is not necessary to obtain approval prior to purchasing property.
b. Yes, all outside business ventures should be cleared through the representative's member firm.
c. Yes, but only if the rental property is located in the same state as the representative's employment.
d. Cannot determine based on the information provided.

67. A customer would like to set up an account with the appropriate trading authorization that would allow for a trustee to make all decisions and enter all orders on behalf of the account's beneficial owners. Which type of account would best suit this objective?

a. Custodial account
b. Discretionary account
c. Fiduciary account
d. Joint account

68. All of the following are requirements that are in place as a result of the Patriot Act EXCEPT:

a. A customer identification program must be utilized to confirm all customer identities.
b. Once the firm suspects any transaction is questionable in nature, it is required to submit a suspicious activity report (SAR).
c. A principal must be assigned by the firm to implement firm policies and oversee employee training.
d. All of the above

69. There are restrictions on the different types of communications member firms can have with the public. Which of the following are meant for a general audience?

I. Websites that require passwords for access
II. Recorded telemarketing messages
III. Postings on the Internet
IV. Printed materials produced for use at a seminar

a. II., III., and IV.
b. III. only
c. II. and III.
d. None of the above

70. A representative is required to obtain certain information from a customer upon opening an account for him. Which of the following is the representative required to update on a regular basis?

a. Customer's net worth
b. Customer's investment objectives
c. Customer bank reference
d. Customer's annual income

71. The business continuity plan regulation is characterized by which of the following statements?

a. The firm must provide for customers to have continued access to their funds.
b. The firm must establish a secondary means for a firm communication system in the event that the primary system is disabled.
c. Two emergency contacts must be appointed from among senior management, one of which must be a registered principal.
d. All of the above

72. A customer comes to her representative requesting to open an account that will be jointly owned between her and another party. Which type of account should the representative recommend if additionally she would like an arrangement that will allow all assets in the account to go to the surviving party in the event of the other's death?

a. Joint tenants with rights of survivorship (JTWROS)
b. Transfer on death (TOD)
c. Joint account
d. Joint tenants in common (JTIC)

73. In establishing an account with a customer who is a US citizen, firms must obtain all of the following EXCEPT:

a. Professional reference and employment verification
b. Social Security number
c. Date of birth
d. Place of business

74. What must a tombstone ad include?

a. Statements that offer further description of the firm's business.
b. Information telling interested parties where they can obtain a prospectus.
c. Various disclaimers made by the firm regarding the offering.
d. Specific details regarding any stockholders meetings that are related to the securities offering.

75. The regulatory portion of the continuing education required of registered agents and principals includes which of the following?

a. They are granted 120 days to complete the required training.
b. As of the agent's second anniversary from their initial registration, they must submit to a computer-based exam.
c. Failure to complete the required training will result in their registration becoming inactive, a subsequent bar from engaging in licensed securities activities, and an inability to receive owed commissions.
d. All of the above

76. All of the following are penalties for being found guilty of insider trading under the Insider Trading and Securities Fraud Enforcement Act of 1988 EXCEPT:

a. A civil fine.
b. Exposure to a lawsuit brought against them by the injured parties.
c. A fine imposed that can be up to a maximum of 300 percent of the amount of financial gain that the guilty party acquired as a result of acting illegally with the insider knowledge.
d. Criminal fine of up to $1,500,000 and 25 years in jail.

77. Which of the following statements are associated with the money-laundering process?

I. “Layering” involves making a variety of deposits, all less than $5,000 each.
II. Launderers buy and sell into and out of the account, and then proceed to reintroduce the funds back into the financial system.
III. Depositing funds with the broker-dealer is the starting point of the process.
IV. “Structuring” involves obtaining funds from a variety of institutions.

a. I., II., III., and IV.
b. I., II., and III.
c. II., III., and IV.
d. II. and III.

78. A registered representative and his client have over time borrowed money from each other. Under industry rules and regulations, are these types of activities allowed to occur?

a. Representatives are prohibited from lending money to their customers.
b. Margin loans are an exception to the restriction on broker-dealers lending to customers.
c. Representatives can borrow money from their customers only if the client is a financial institution and actively in the business of doing so.
d. All of the above

79. Which organization was established to provide aid in the event of the failure of a broker-dealer?

a. The Securities Investor Protection Corporation
b. Unit Investment Trust
c. Subchapter S Corporation
d. None of the above

80. Under certain conditions, a representative can continue to receive commissions post-retirement. Given that, all of the following are true of representatives after retirement EXCEPT:

a. Upon the death of a representative, her beneficiaries can continue to receive any commissions still owed to that representative.
b. They may receive commissions on new business as long as it came as a result of a referral from a client they had pre-retirement.
c. A contract regarding future commissions signed prior to retirement is necessary in order to receive commissions on business that occurs post-retirement.
d. Finder's fees are not given to retired representatives post-retirement.

81. Which of the following statements accurately depicts a regulation that a firm must abide by in relation to the telemarketing calls makes to consumers?

a. It is required to provide clear and thorough procedures regarding the use and maintenance of the Do Not Call list.
b. Calls are restricted to the hours between 9 a.m. and 8 p.m.
c. Once individuals are entered onto the Do Not Call list, the firm must refrain from calling them for three years.
d. All of the above

82. Insider trading is considered a violation of:

a. Investment Company Act of 1940
b. Investment Advisers Act of 1940
c. Blue-sky laws
d. Securities Exchange Act of 1934

83. Of the following types of communication that are available to member firms for use when communicating with the public, which one is utilized for a more targeted audience?

a. Member firm research reports
b. Billboards
c. Magazine content
d. All of the above

84. Institutional investors:

I. May include employment benefit plans with participants of all sizes and numbers.
II. Can be an individual or a firm.
III. May be an insurance company.
IV. Actively trade securities only for the accounts of others.

a. II. and III.
b. I., II., and III.
c. III. only
d. II., III., and IV.

85. Considering a member firm's use of testimonials, all of the statements below are true EXCEPT:

a. If individuals outside of the firm are responsible for the creation and content of the distributed materials, their names must be disclosed.
b. Any references made to past firm performance must include statements qualifying that future performance is not necessarily ensured based on success having been achieved in the past.
c. Statements by individuals do not require specific designation of expert status or not.
d. Must disclose if the individual whose testimonial was used was compensated for his participation.

86. All of the following individuals are exempt from FINRA registration EXCEPT:

a. FINRA firm member employee, newly graduated, four months working at the firm, and participating in limited security sales to customers.
b. FINRA firm member employees who are officers having no supervisory responsibilities or contact with customers.
c. FINRA firm member employee whose sole responsibilities are clerical in nature.
d. Those individuals having no US citizenship and working abroad.

87. Firms utilize generic advertising in order to promote the services and products they provide. The content of this type of advertising usually includes all of the following EXCEPT:

a. Types of accounts that the firm offers to their customers
b. Firm's securities products
c. Firm's contact information
d. Directed investment advice

88. Which of the following types of communication between registered members and the public can be described as written communication to investors in numbers of 25 or more within a 30-day period of time?

a. Correspondence
b. Retail communications
c. Institutional communications
d. None of the above

89. FINRA member firms have an obligation to provide continued education on industry topics to their covered employees by doing which of the following?

I. The instituted training plan must be formally filed with FINRA.
II. The firm must identify the needs of their employees and implement a training plan at least every two years.
III. The training offered to covered employees should have particular focus given to the products specific to the firm, as well as the risks that go along with them.
IV. Their failure to comply with documenting their training and continuing education plans is under penalty of disciplinary action.

a. I., III., and IV.
b. I., II., and III.
c. III. and IV.
d. I., II., III., and IV.

90. Choose which of the following statements is TRUE of retail communications.

a. All online interactions made by registered members that have any connection to the securities industry cannot be initiated without first getting a principal's approval.
b. Advertisements are not included in this category of communications.
c. A registered principal must approve this type of communication before its initial distribution to the public.
d. This type of communication must be maintained by the registered member for two years.

91. An individual applying for FINRA registration can be found to be ineligible for all of the following reasons EXCEPT:

a. If it is found that she submitted false or misleading information on her Form U-4.
b. If she had a securities-related felony conviction at any time in the last 12 years.
c. If she was the primary cause of a broker-dealer being suspended.
d. If the individual is barred from registration due to a court order.

92. FINRA rule 2210 reduced the categories of communication allowed between registered members and the public. Which of the following are categories of communication under the current rule?

a. Correspondence
b. Institutional communications
c. Retail communications
d. All of the above

93. Which of the following statements are TRUE of the Insider Trading and Securities Fraud Enforcement Act of 1988?

I. The spouse of an insider is also considered to be a company insider.
II. Provides guidelines regarding the distribution of material company information to individuals who are outside of the company.
III. An insider can include a stockholder with 5 percent ownership.
IV. It is illegal for insiders to utilize nonpublic material company information to benefit from profits related to the company's stock.

a. II., III., and IV.
b. IV. only
c. I., II., and IV.
d. II. and IV.

94. With regards to the "gift rule," if an employee were to accept a gift from another broker-dealer, what is he then required to do in relation to the gift?

a. Submit a form detailing the gift and its dollar value.
b. Acquire a record of the gift to include the names of both the giver and who received it, and then the purpose and nature of the gift.
c. Send a message to the giver confirming receipt of the gift.
d. Obtain his supervisor's approval for the gift.

95. A husband and wife would like to set up a Uniform Gifts to Minors Act (UGMA) account for their three children. All of the following are true of their options to do so EXCEPT:

a. As the parents and legal guardians of the three children, they have the ability and authority to act as custodians of an account for the benefit of all of them.
b. They may not act as custodians together over a single UGMA account.
c. Each of the three children must have his or her own individual UGMA accounts.
d. One parent may act as custodian over multiple UGMA accounts.

96. A representative has acquired a new account for which he must make appropriate investment recommendations. In speaking to the new client, which of the following topics should he obtain information on prior to making his recommendations?

a. Their retirement plans and the financial objectives needed to support them.
b. Their other investment holdings.
c. Extent to which they have large current expenses such as college.
d. All of the above

97. A registered representative has a customer who passes away. Given that there are certain guidelines for how to handle such a situation, the representative should do all of the following EXCEPT:

a. Maintain a hold on the account until contacted by the executor of the customer's estate with further instructions.
b. Continue to trade on the account per the customer's last instructions based on the discretionary authority previously granted to him by the customer.
c. Upon receiving notice of the customer's death, mark the account as "deceased" and cancel all open orders.
d. Attempt to obtain a certified copy of the customer's death certificate.

98. Which of the following should a representative seeking to meet the investment objectives of her customer initially review and then continue to maintain over time?

a. The type and timing of growth they would like to see their money have.
b. Their specific income needs.
c. The extent to which they are willing to lose money in order to make money.
d. All of the above

99. A representative has had an account for which he was given discretionary authority as of the opening of the account. He has continued as the account representative for three years and two months. Which of the following is TRUE of this representative as it pertains to his position relative to this account?

a. The representative has the authority to transfer discretion to another employee of their firm in the event that he is unavailable to trade on behalf of their customer.
b. The representative continues to have discretion over the account based on the original power of attorney the customer signed as of the opening of the account.
c. Assuming the representative still has discretionary authority, he would have sole authority over the account as the customer is no longer able to enter orders.
d. If given a full power of attorney, he would have the authority to transact cash and securities in and out of the account.

100. In 2025, a minor receives as birthday gifts four separate monetary gifts from each of his parents, his grandfather, and his uncle. Which of the following gifts into his Uniform Gift to Minors Act account (UGMA) is considered by the IRS as tax-free?

Father's gift:	$8,000
Mother's gift:	$6,000
Grandfather's gift:	$20,000
Uncle's gift:	$13,000

I. Father
II. Mother
III. Grandfather
IV. Uncle

a. I., II., III., and IV.
b. I., II., and IV.
c. II. only.
d. I. and II.

Answers and Explanations

1. D: All of the above are Civil Judicial Disclosures that are required by FINRA Rule 8312. The disclosures specifically involving former associates registered on or after August 16, 1999, party to an investment-related civil action initiated by a financial regulatory authority, state or foreign, and dismissed as the result of a settlement agreement are the result of a recent 8312 rule change.

2. C: FINRA Rule 1250 is associated with continuing education requirements. FINRA Rule 2266 is associated with the disclosure of SIPC (Securities Investment Protection Corporation) information, FINRA Rule 11870 is associated with customer account transfer contracts, and FINRA Rule 1122 is associated with the filing of misleading information regarding membership or registration.

3. B: Per FINRA Rule 3220, members are required to keep separate records of all gifts and gratuities, and there is an exclusion for any payments that are made related to authentic written contracts for employment. Members' gifts or gratuities made in relation to the business of the employer of the person who receives it must not exceed $100 per year.

4. A: A broker using the standard of "reasonableness" when determining whether a series of proposed securities transactions are not excessive in relation to a particular account is quantitative suitability. A broker considering the specific customer's investment profile when determining, using a "reasonableness" standard, the suitability of a security transaction or investment strategy for that customer is customer-specific suitability. A broker, in determining that a given security transaction or investment strategy is suitable for at least "some" investors, and exercising reasonable diligence in researching and understanding the proposed security transaction or investment strategy, is reasonable-basis suitability.

5. C: In order for a member firm to be allowed to compensate non-registered foreign persons for business directed to them by said foreign persons, several conditions must be met, some of which include the customer being provided a document detailing the compensation paid to the finders, the finders being either foreign nationals or foreign entities living abroad, and the transaction confirmation specifying the finder's fee paid.

6. A: Characteristics of the term "security" include being easily transferred between two parties, being traded for some value, and primarily being either debt or equity. Lastly, a security MUST BE subject to some risk.

7. B: Exchange-traded funds, mutual funds, and variable annuities are all examples of securities. Fixed annuities are NOT securities in that they carry no risk, given that principal and earnings are guaranteed by the insurance company contracted to provide payments.

8. C: Securities, property, and accounts receivable are all considered assets. Accounts payable is NOT considered to be an asset and is instead one of the liabilities listed on a balance sheet.

9. B: Outstanding stock is sold to the public and then remains "outstanding" with investors, having NOT been purchased back by the corporation. Treasury stock is that which is sold to the public and then repurchased by the issuing corporation. Authorized stock is the largest number of shares of stock that the corporation is authorized to sell to the public, as determined during its process of incorporation.

10. A: The formula for calculating a corporation's amount of treasury stock based on the amounts given is:

$$\text{Issued Stock} - \text{Outstanding Stock} = \text{Treasury Stock}$$

$$73{,}000 - 51{,}000 = 22{,}000$$

11. C: In a rights offering, a shareholder will have the "right" and opportunity to purchase new additional shares at the subscription price, not book value. The subscription price is less than the stock's current market value and is good for 45 days. Additionally, in a rights offering, a shareholder may exercise his rights, sell his rights, or allow them to expire.

12. B: Shareholders as investors in a corporation possess the right to inspect the corporation's books and records and participate in votes regarding mergers, acquisitions, stocks splits, and the election of the board of directors. They do NOT have the right to review what the corporation deems "confidential" financial data.

13. A: The settlement date of a securities transaction between two investors is the date when recorded ownership of the security is officially transferred to the new owner of the security. The payment date is the due date for payment to be made for the purchased security. The declaration date actually has nothing to do with the security transaction process, but is instead the date that a corporation's board of directors makes the decision to declare a dividend payment to its common shareholders. The trade date is the date of the actual execution of the security transaction order, which can be different from the date the order was originally placed.

14. D: There are many consequences a customer must endure as a result of violating Regulation T, some of which include the subject securities of the violation being sold, a requirement that money be deposited in the account up front for any purchases intended within the next 90 days, and the customer's account being sold out and frozen.

15. D: Participating preferred stock provides the shareholder who possesses it the right to receive both preferred and common dividends that are paid out. Cumulative preferred stock allows for dividends to accumulate in arrears, provided the corporation cannot pay them for some period of time. Convertible preferred stock offers its shareholders the opportunity to convert their shares into common shares at a fixed price. Noncumulative preferred stock provides the investor nothing other than the preferred dividend rate payment.

16. C: $\frac{\text{par value}}{\text{conversion price}} = \text{\# of common shares}$

$$\frac{\$100}{\$10} = 10$$

17. B: All of the statements are true EXCEPT registered representatives are not allowed to utilize the anticipated payment of a dividend on a stock as the sole reason for recommending the purchase of that stock. Doing so would be committing a violation.

18. A: Warrants provide an investor the opportunity to buy common stock at a specific subscription price, and the offer to do so may last up to 10 years. Calls and puts are types of option contracts that provide investors the opportunity to buy or sell a security at a specific price, for a specific period of time.

19. D: Warrants can be obtained through a bond offering, as a "unit" resulting from participation in an initial public offering, and by purchasing them in the secondary market.

20. C: All of the statements regarding options are true EXCEPT the seller of an option contract does NOT retain the right to decline the transaction contracted for. The seller of an option contract is obligated to buy or sell (depending on the type of contract sold) on the contract once payment of the premium from the buyer of the contract is received.

21. D: An investor with a bullish outlook towards a security would generally believe in its ability to increase in value and accordingly may sell put options or buy call options in order to benefit from that increase.

22. B: The option contract provides the investor with the opportunity to buy PRK @ $45 per share. The $7 amount is how much the investor paid for the OPTION to buy one round lot of 100 shares of PRK ($700 total) @ $45 per share. The 1 above represents the one round lot of 100 shares of PRK that the investor has the opportunity to purchase through the option contract.

23. A: A firm acting as a broker executes orders and receives a commission for doing so. A firm acting as a dealer fills customer's orders by selling from or buying for their own account, and acting as a market maker.

24. C: All of the statements are true of corporate bondholders EXCEPT that they are NOT owners of the corporation but are instead creditors of it.

25. B: The US government is the largest issuer of debt.

26. A: Book entry bonds are not evidenced by an actual physical certificate; instead, proof of ownership comes from the trade confirmation for the transaction. Principal-only registration bonds and bearer bonds are issued with physical bond certificates.

27. D: All of these terms can be used interchangeably with the term par value and in fact they all represent an amount equal to $1,000.

28. C: The formula for quoting the price of a corporate bond is:

$$\text{percentage of par} \times \$1{,}000$$

$$\mathbf{98.74\% \times \$1,000 = \$987.40}$$

29. B: A bond's nominal yield is fixed, printed on the bond at issuance, and is known as its coupon rate. A bond's yield to maturity is the total annualized return that is received by the individual investing in it. The current yield is the bond's annual income divided by its current market price.

30. A: For a given bond investment, as its price rises, its yield will fall demonstrating the inverse relationship the two have with each other. Accordingly, as the price falls, the yield will rise.

31. C:

$$\text{nominal yield} \times \$1{,}000 = \text{annual income}$$

$$\text{percentage of par} \times \$1{,}000 = \text{current market price}$$

$$\frac{\text{bond's annual income}}{\text{bond's current market price}} = \text{current yield}$$

$$7\% \times \$1{,}000 = \$70 \quad \text{annual income}$$

$$105\% \times \$1{,}000 = \$1{,}050 \quad \text{current market price}$$

$$\frac{\$70}{\$1{,}050} = .0667 = 6.67\% \quad \text{current yield}$$

32. B: Equipment trust certificates, collateral trust certificates, and mortgage bonds are all secured bonds and are backed by assets that are held as collateral by bondholders as protection against the risk of default. Debentures are UNSECURED bonds, are NOT backed by collateral assets, and are simply backed by the good faith and credit of the organization issuing them.

33. A: Zero coupon bonds do NOT pay semiannual interest, but ARE taxed for annual appreciation, are issued at a price discounted to par, and have the most price sensitivity to changes in interest rates.

34. B: Convertible bond conversion formula:

$$\frac{\text{par value}}{\text{conversion price}} = \text{\# of shares upon conversion}$$

Note: Par value for bonds is $1,000.

$$\frac{\$1{,}000}{\$5} = 200 \text{ shares}$$

35. C: Convertible preferred stock conversion formula:

$$\frac{\text{par value}}{\text{conversion price}} = \text{\# of shares upon conversion}$$

Note: Par value for preferred stock is $100.

$$\frac{\$100}{\$20} = 5 \text{ shares}$$

36. A: Convertible bond conversion formula:

$$\frac{\text{par value}}{\text{conversion price}} = \text{\# of shares upon conversion}$$

Note: Par value for bonds is $1,000.

$$\frac{\text{current market value of the bond}}{\text{\# of converted shares}} = \text{parity price}$$

$$\frac{\$1{,}000}{\$50} = 20 \text{ shares upon conversion}$$

$$\frac{\$1{,}750}{20} = \$87.50 \quad \text{parity price}$$

37. D: Treasury bills do NOT pay semiannual interest. They are awarded via weekly auctions, have maturities between 4 to 52 weeks, and are priced at a discount from par.

38. D: Series EE and Series HH are both nonmarketable government securities and accordingly are exclusively sold and redeemed by the government; treasury STRIPS and receipts are NOT.

39. B: GNMA (the Government National Mortgage Association) is the only agency with securities that are backed by the full faith and credit of the US government utilizing pools of mortgages that are insured by the Federal Housing Administration and the Department of Veteran Affairs. FHLMC (the Federal Home Loan Mortgage Corporation) and FNMA (the Federal National Mortgage Association) both utilize mortgages and mortgage pools that are NOT.

40. C: FNMA and FHLMC are both publicly traded corporations. GNMA is a government corporation and a CMO is a type of mortgage-backed security.

41. A: FNMA is in the business of purchasing mortgages with the intent to then bundle them as mortgage-backed securities. FNMA is NOT known as Fannie Mac but instead Fannie Mae, creates securities that produce interest income that are fully taxable, and provides notes that are issued in denominations ranging from $5,000 to $1,000,000.

42. B: The primary investment risk facing owners of CMOs is early refinancing that results in them being paid sooner than they had originally planned for. Although a change in interest rates affects homeowners' inclination to refinance either sooner or later, the change itself is NOT the primary investment risk that refinancing is. Interest and principal are paid monthly in a structured format tranche by tranche, and although the rate of payments may vary, the risk of "late" payments is not an issue.

43. D: There actually is a secondary market for most CMOs, these securities are backed by pools of mortgages, and a rise in interest rates can realistically cause a slowing of refinancing activity and, accordingly, a slowing in repayments to investors based on the structured repayment schedule established for the security.

44. C: General obligation bonds are backed by the full faith and credit of the issuing organization and its ability to obtain taxes to repay the obligations to investors. Revenue bonds are used to fund projects that produce revenue and, accordingly, the debt obligations are funded by that revenue. Industrial development bonds are issued on behalf of a private corporation with the result being that lease payments paid by the corporation provide the funding for the debt obligations.

45. D:

$$\frac{\text{yield of tax} - \text{free bond}}{(100\% - \text{investor's tax bracket})} = \text{tax equivalent yield}$$

$$\frac{5\%}{(100\% - 22\%)} = \frac{5\%}{78\%} = .064 = 6.4\%$$

Further, the investor would be better to invest in the municipal bond if the corporate bond of comparable quality does not yield more than the 6.4 percent.

46. D: If the municipal bond is purchased within the investor's state of residence, the interest earned will be FREE of federal, state, and local taxes.

47. A: Federal funds loans are NOT government money market instruments; they are corporate money market instruments. Short-term discount notes, treasury securities with less than one year left, and treasury bills can all be categorized as government money market instruments.

48. C: The Federal Deposit Insurance Corporation (FDIC) insures the first $250,000 of a negotiable CD, although denominations are issued beyond $1,000,000.

49. B: Commercial paper is an unsecured promissory note that is issued at a discount of face value and has maturities ranging from 1 to 270 days. Negotiable certificates of deposit, not commercial paper, have set maturities that range from 30 days to 10+ years.

50. D: While opening and servicing customers' accounts, a firm may ask questions regarding their net worth, investment objectives, and employment status; however, before opening an account, the firm is REQUIRED to obtain the customer's date of birth.

51. A: Once FINRA notifies a member of a complaint against it, it has only 25 days to provide its written response, not 60. FINRA can dismiss allegations if they're found to be without merit, routinely review member firms, and choose to have a formal hearing as a means to resolve an allegation.

52. D: All of the above are true of the minor rule violation process.

53. B: FINRA's possible penalties for member rule violations include the member being barred for life and censure. A fine may be imposed for any amount, and the suspension is for only up to one year, not five.

54. A: Decisions resulting from FINRA member violation investigations must be appealed to the National Adjudicatory Counsel (NAC) within 15 days of the decision.

55. C: FINRA's code of arbitration states that customers, upon agreeing to arbitration as their choice for dispute resolution, must do so in writing. Industry members, however, are REQUIRED to use arbitration to settle disputes. It is NOT required as an industry standard to have customers sign customer agreements upon opening accounts, although they often do so. The statute of limitations for arbitration is actually six years from time of the event in dispute.

56. D: Registered representatives, customers, and banks can all utilize arbitration as a choice of dispute resolution versus members.

57. B: Arbitration awards are final and NOT available for appeal. Monetary payments are required to be paid within 30 days, and failure to pay awards imposes a penalty of suspension.

58. C: Mediation provides for one of three conclusions, which are mutual agreement, impasse with no resolution, or individuals withdrawing from the process. Simplified arbitration provides for a decision handed out by a single arbitrator. Panel arbitration provides for a decision to be made by an odd-numbered panel of arbitrators.

59. A: Settlement date for government bond transactions is the next business day after the trade date. ALL cash-basis trades settle on the same day as the trade date, and all "regular-way" transactions (common and preferred stock, corporate bonds, etc.) settle three business days after the trade date.

60. D: The Federal Reserve Board, not the SEC, is responsible for regulating payment dates under Regulation T. Payment date is five business days after trade date. Payment date is when monetary payment is due for securities purchased, and firms do have the authority to require payment from their customers sooner than five days after trade date.

61. D: Variable annuities have portfolios that include stocks and mutual fund shares. Additionally, they are NOT susceptible to the risk of inflation, representatives need to obtain BOTH an insurance and securities license to sell to customers, and the return is NOT guaranteed.

62. B: Regulation S-P was created as an extension of the privacy rules of the Graham-Leach-Bliley Act. The Investment Advisers Act of 1940 provides guidelines for investment advisers. The Employee Retirement Income Security Act of 1974 regulates private-sector pension plans.

63. C: The method that would be best for this investor would be the hold in street name method that involves having the investor be the beneficial owner of the securities and the firm the nominal owner. Transfer and ship simply means the securities are registered in the investor's name and then sent to them directly. Transfer and hold in safekeeping involves the securities being registered in the investor's name but then held with the firm.

64. B: The protection provided to brokerage customers is by customer, not account. Per customer, the cash coverage is up $250,000. Therefore, given the information provided, customers C and D will be provided full cash coverage from the SIPC.

65. D: Given a joint account between a customer and a representative, the representative can share in the profits of that account as long as the firm approves the account prior to its opening, only if they actually invest funds into the account, and in proportion to the amount they invest into the account.

66. A: A registered representative is NOT required to obtain approval from her firm prior to purchasing rental property. It IS necessary that she receive approval from her employer for all outside business ventures EXCEPT participating as a passive investor in a business and investing in rental property.

67. C: A fiduciary account will allow for a trustee to make all order decisions on the account on behalf of the account's beneficial owners. A custodial account allows for a custodian, as the nominal owner, to enter account orders on behalf of a minor, the beneficial owner. A discretionary account provides for a registered representative to be given limited authority to execute orders on the account. A joint account is an account with two or more adult owners.

68. B: The Patriot Act requires that firms ONLY submit a suspicious activity report (SAR) for questionable transactions above $5,000. They are also required to utilize a customer identification program to confirm customer identities, and assign a principal to implement firm policies regarding the detection of suspicious activity.

69. C: Member firm communications meant for a general audience include recorded telemarketing messages and postings on the Internet. Password-accessed websites and printed seminar materials are meant for a more targeted audience.

70. B: Representatives must maintain their customer's account by regularly updating their investment objectives. Although they obtain their customers' net worth, bank reference, and annual income during the process of opening their account, they do NOT need to regularly confirm or update that account information on an ongoing basis.

71. D: The business continuity plan regulation requires a firm to ensure customer access to funds, establish a secondary communication system in the event the primary one is disabled, and provide for two emergency contacts to be communicated to FINRA via their continuity plan.

72. A: A joint tenants with rights of survivorship (JTWROS) account is a jointly owned account that allows for a surviving party to receive all assets within the account in the event of the death of the other party. A transfer on death (TOD) account would allow the owner of the account to assign a beneficiary that will receive all assets from the account in the event of the owner's death. A joint account is simply one that is owned by two or more adults. A joint tenants in common (JTIC) account provides that in the event of one owner's death, their portion of the account goes to their estate, and does not get assigned to the other owner of the account.

73. A: In establishing an account, US customers must submit to the broker-dealer their Social Security number, date of birth, and place of business. They are NOT required to submit a professional reference or employment verification.

74. B: A tombstone ad MUST include information directing those interested where to get a prospectus. It MAY include descriptions of the business, firm disclaimers, and information regarding stockholders meetings.

75. D: The regulatory continuing education required of agents must be completed within 120 days from notice to comply. It is a computer-based exam and failure to comply will result in the agent's registration becoming inactive.

76. D: Individuals found guilty of insider trading can have imposed on them a criminal fine of up to $1,000,000, not $1,500,000, and face a sentence of up to 10 years in jail, not 25. Additional penalties may include a civil fine, exposure to a lawsuit by the injured parties, and a fine of up to 300 percent of the gain gotten through the illegal use of the insider information.

77. C: The money-laundering process starts with depositing funds with the broker-dealer. The individuals utilize structuring by obtaining the funds from different institutions, and they then proceed to buy and sell into and out of the account, ultimately moving to then reintroduce the funds back into the financial system. Layering through multiple deposits of $10,000 or less is utilized also.

78. D: A lending relationship between a representative and a customer is allowable under certain conditions. Representatives may NOT provide financial loans to customers; however, broker-dealers can provide margin loans. Representatives may ONLY borrow money from a customer if the customer is a financial institution and in the business of actively providing loans.

79. A: The Securities Investor Protection Corporation was established to protect customers in the event of the failure of a broker-dealer. A unit investment trust is a type of investment organization that invests in securities within a portfolio. A subchapter S corporation provides for the owners of the organization to be held responsible for the tax consequences of that organization.

80. B: There are NO commissions given to retired representatives on any new business that occurs AFTER their retirement. Upon their death, beneficiaries can receive previously retired representatives' applicable commissions, a contract in place is required for post-retirement commissions to be collected, and retired representatives may NOT receive finder's fees post-retirement.

81. A: Firms must provide clear and thorough procedures regarding the use and maintenance of their Do Not Call list. Telemarketing calls are restricted to between the hours of 8 a.m. and 9 p.m. (NOT 9 a.m. and 8 p.m.), and once entered onto the Do Not Call list, customers may not be contacted by the firm for five years, NOT three.

82. D: Insider trading is a violation of the Securities Exchange Act of 1934. The Investment Company Act of 1940 is related to investment firms and specifically their operations and registration. The Investment Advisers Act of 1940 is related to investment advisers and any requirements associated with them. Blue-sky laws are associated with an offering's registration process, specifically at the state level.

83. A: Member firm research reports are meant for a more targeted audience. Billboards and magazine content are for a general audience.

84. A: Institutional investors may be an individual or firm, and can be an insurance company. Institutional investors may also include employment benefit plans, but only those with 100 or more participants. Institutional investors may trade securities for others, but can also trade on behalf of their own account.

85. C: If individuals used to provide a testimonial are considered to be experts in their field, disclosures detailing their qualifications for doing so must be provided. Materials sourced from individuals outside of the firm must have their names disclosed, disclosures must be made clarifying that references to past performance do NOT indicate future performance, and disclosures regarding compensation for testimony must also be made.

86. A: ANYONE participating in securities sales to customers, limited or otherwise, is subject to the requirement to first obtain FINRA registration. Those who are exempt include non-supervisory officers who participate in no customer contact, those whose role is solely clerical, and non-US citizens who are working abroad.

87. D: A firm's generic advertising will NOT usually include specific and directed investment advice. It WILL usually include the types of accounts the firm offers, the securities products it specializes in, and its contact information.

88. B: Retail communication is directed at 25 or MORE retail investors and occurs within a 30-day period of time. Correspondence involves communications initiated by registered members and directed at LESS than 25 investors that comes in written OR electronic form, and within a 30-day period. Institutional communications are those that occur strictly between registered members and institutional investors.

89. C: FINRA members should have a formal plan to train their employees on both the products specific to their firm as well as the risks of those products. Their failure to provide such training is under penalty of disciplinary action. They are NOT required to file a formal plan with FINRA, unless asked to do so. They are required to identify the needs of their employees and implement a training plan, but it should be at least every year, not every two.

90. C: All retail communications must be approved by a registered principal prior to their initial distribution to the public. Online interactions made by registered members are exempt from principal approval UNLESS they involve specific promotion of the firm's business, or contain actual investment advice. Advertisements ARE considered to be retail communications. Retail communications must be maintained by the registered member for three years, not two.

91. B: This individual would be ineligible for registration if it was found he or she had a securities-related felony conviction anytime in the last 10 years, not 12. She would be ineligible also if she had submitted false or misleading information about herself, had caused a broker-dealer's suspension, or had been barred from registration due to a court order.

92. D: FINRA rule 2210 reduced the communication categories from six to three. The three categories are correspondence, institutional communications, and retail communications.

93. C: The Insider Trading and Securities Fraud Enforcement Act of 1988 considers an insider's spouse to also be an insider, provides guidelines regarding the distribution of material company information to those outside of the company, and makes it illegal for insiders to use nonpublic material company information to make a profit on the movements of the company stock. It also states that an insider may be a stockholder with 10 percent ownership, NOT 5 percent.

94. B: The gift rule states that the recipient of the gift acquires a record of the gift detailing the giver's name, the recipient's name and the nature of the gift. It is NOT a requirement of the gift rule that the recipient submits a form with the gift's dollar value, sends a message confirming receipt of the gift, or obtains his supervisor's approval.

95. A: Per the Uniform Gifts to Minors Act, the two parents here may NOT act as custodians together over one individual account. Further, each minor child must have his or her own individual account. It is also true that if necessary, one parent MAY act as custodian over one or more of the children's UGMA accounts.

96. D: In order to make appropriate investment objectives for this customer, the representative should review the client's retirement plans, investment holdings, and current expenses, specifically large ones such as college tuition.

97. B: In the event of a customer's death, a representative should NOT continue to trade on the account due to their discretionary authority having automatically ended as of the customer's death. He SHOULD maintain a hold on the account while waiting for further instructions from the estate, cancel all orders, mark the account as "deceased", and try to obtain a certified copy of the customer's death certificate.

98. D: Representatives should initially discuss with their customers, and then continually review over time, their expectations for financial growth, income needs, and expectations for retaining and losing money.

99. D: A FULL power of attorney would grant the representative the authority to transact securities and cash in and out of the customer's account. The representative may NOT transfer his discretionary authority to someone else. His discretionary authority would no longer be in effect due to the original signed power of attorney being MORE than three years old. Even if the representative's discretionary authority was still in effect, the customer ALWAYS retains the ability to enter orders on his own account.

100. B: Per the IRS, the size limit for tax-free gifts to minors into a Uniform Gifts to Minors account (UGMA) is $19,000 per year (2025). Accordingly, the father's gift of $8,000, the mother's gift of $6,000, and the uncle's gift of $13,000 are all considered tax-free. The grandfather's gift of $20,000 is NOT considered tax-free.

Practice Test #2

1. An investor is looking to generate income without taking on significant market risk. She wants a debt security that is investment grade but still pays a high coupon. Assuming she has $10,000 to invest, which of the following positions would fulfill her goals? Also calculate the value of each coupon payment.

a. AA rated ABC corp. bonds 101 4% coupon – $40.4 each payment
b. CC rated XYZ corp. bonds 97 7% coupon – $67.9 each payment
c. US Treasury Bonds 101 5% coupon – $25 each payment
d. Municipal Bonds 104 4% coupon – $41.6 each payment

2. Place the following mutual fund dividend distribution dates in the order in which they occur.

I. Payment date
II. Record date
III. Declaration date
IV. Ex-dividend date

a. II., III., I., and IV.
b. III., II., IV., and I.
c. III., II., I., and IV.
d. I., II., III., and IV.

3. Which of the following statements are true regarding letters of intent?

I. Can be backdated to include a previous purchase as long as it's within the prior 90 days.
II. Affords the investor up to 12 months to meet the investment level she is committing to subscribe to.
III. Provides that if the investor fails to reach the subscribed level, the sales charge is simply adjusted upward.
IV. Acts as a binding contract for the investor.

a. II., III., and IV.
b. III. and IV.
c. I., II., and III.
d. I. and III.

4. Open-end funds charge a sales charge as a cost of distribution. What is the maximum amount they can charge as a percentage of the public offering price (POP)?

a. 5.5 percent
b. 9 percent
c. 8.5 percent
d. 7 percent

5. An investor would like to invest within a family of funds by moving his money from fund EF to fund DC. Fund EF's shares have a net asset value (NAV) of $9.50 and a public offering price (POP) of $10.25, and fund DC's shares have a net asset value (NAV) of $19.10 and a public offering price (POP) of $19.95. Given that conversion privileges are provided by this fund, at what price will this investor both redeem and purchase the proposed shares?

a. Fund EF at $9.50, fund DC at $19.10
b. Fund EF at $10.25, fund DC at $19.95
c. Fund EF at $9.88, fund DC at $19.52
d. None of the above

6. A money market fund will invest in:

a. Debt securities with maturities of less than 1 year
b. Commercial paper
c. Banker's acceptances
d. All of the above

7. Utilizing the information given, calculate the net asset value (NAV) per share for mutual fund BC.

Assets:	$25,000,000
Liabilities:	$2,200,000
Shares outstanding:	4,500,000

a. $5.07
b. $6.04
c. $10.36
d. $5.56

8. Which of the following statements describes the primary difference between rights of accumulation and a letter of intent?

a. The sales charge reduction does not apply to previous investment purchases.
b. There is no time limit on rights of accumulation.
c. Investors can qualify for a reduction in sales charge based on past investments.
d. In calculating whether the investor qualifies, current investments are considered.

9. How can an investor determine her cost base given that she owns a large sum of shares purchased through different transactions?

a. Share identification
b. First in, first out
c. Average cost
d. All of the above

10. Which of these statements are accurate requirements for a mutual fund prospectus?

a. Sixteen months after publication, the prospectus should be disposed of.
b. The fund is required to update the information in the prospectus every 12 months.
c. The fund should, but is not required to, update the information in the prospectus every 6 months.
d. The fund prospectus can be available for use and distribution for up to 18 months from publication.

11. What is the total capital gain or loss for an investor who purchased 2,500 shares of a mutual fund at $17 per share and then sold them at $14 per share?

a. $7,500 capital gain
b. $7,500 capital loss
c. $2,500 capital loss
d. $2,500 capital gain

12. Which of the following is the formula for determining the net investment income of a mutual fund?

a. Capital gains + dividend income - expenses
b. Average net assets + interest income + dividend income - expenses
c. Dividend income + interest income + capital gains - expenses
d. Capital gains + interest income - expenses

13. Given the following information on mutual fund BC, calculate its front-end load sales charge on an investment of $25,000.

NAV:	$7.45
Sales charge percent:	6.5 percent

a. $1,625
b. $487.50
c. $336
d. $384

14. An investor invests into a family of funds, investing $15,000 into an equity portfolio and $12,000 into a sector portfolio. The breakpoint schedule for the family of funds states that the sales charge for investments up to $25,000 is 9.5 percent, and the sales charge for just above $25,000 is a reduced 7 percent. Given the amount invested, at which rate will the $27,000 investment purchase be charged?

a. 7 percent
b. 8 percent
c. 9.5 percent
d. Cannot determine, need more information

15. An investment company's full notice of registration to the SEC must include:

a. Officers and directors biographical info
b. Investment concentration
c. Known plans for borrowing
d. All of the above

16. Which of the following statements is TRUE regarding reinvesting capital gains and dividend distributions?

a. It is possible that a service charge may be incurred at the point of reinvestment of each distribution.
b. Some funds allow investors to reinvest at the net asset value (NAV) or at a discount to the public purchase price (POP)
c. Whether reinvested or not, all distributions are taxed.
d. All of the above

17. Mutual fund shares may be distributed through different avenues. Which involves the mutual fund selling its shares directly to investors at the net asset value (NAV) price?

a. Selling group
b. No-load mutual fund
c. Underwriter
d. None of the above

18. Which of the following statements are TRUE in relation to investors being given conversion privileges within a mutual fund of families?

a. Investors redeem shares at the NAV to then utilize the proceeds for buying shares in a second portfolio (within the same family of funds) also at the NAV.
b. Investors are waived a sales charge when exchanging money between portfolios within the same fund family if done within 30 days.
c. No commissions can be paid for this transaction.
d. All of the above

19. Given mutual fund BC, which of the following situational occurrences will NOT affect a change in its NAV?

a. Dividends being distributed to investors.
b. Securities being purchased or sold within the portfolio.
c. Securities' prices, and thus values, increasing or decreasing according to market fluctuations.
d. Bond interest payments are infused into the portfolio.

20. Which TWO statements below are restrictions that apply to money market funds?

I. Investments must carry one of the top two ratings given by the primary industry rating agencies.
II. Portfolio securities must have an average maturity of not more than 180 days.
III. Assets must not exceed 8 percent in any single issuer's securities.
IV. Portfolio securities may not have maturities of more than 13 months.

a. I. and III.
b. I. and IV.
c. II. and IV.
d. II. and III.

21. A back-end load is a charge that an investor pays at the point of redeeming shares and the amount decreases the longer the investor puts off redeeming those shares. What is another name for this charge?

a. Level load sales charge
b. Contingent deferred sales charge
c. Asset-based fee
d. None of the above

22. The Investment Company Act of 1940 states that there are three types of investment companies. Which one can be described as investing in either a fixed or non-fixed portfolio of securities, not actively managed, and offering shares to investors that provide for an undivided interest in those securities?

a. Face-amount company
b. Unit investment trust (UIT)
c. Real estate investment trust
d. Management investment companies (mutual funds)

23. An investor is looking into investing in mutual fund BC. How would he calculate the sales charge percentage, given that he only knows the fund's Net asset value (NAV) and public offering price (POP)?

Net asset value (NAV):	$8.00
Public offering price (POP):	$8.50

a. 9.4 percent
b. 6.3 percent
c. 5.9 percent
d. 5 percent

24. All of the following are true of bond funds EXCEPT:

a. Examples of bond funds include municipal, government, and corporate.
b. Bond fund investments are essentially an investment in a portfolio of debt.
c. Main focus is to pass along to investors income by way of interest payments.
d. Government bond fund dividends are not subject to taxes.

25. The type of prospectus that details information such as a balance sheet and income statement is:

a. Advertising prospectus
b. Summary prospectus
c. Statement of additional information
d. None of the above

26. There are several different types of mutual funds based on the type of investment objective set forth by the fund. Which type of fund can be described as having its investments in stocks and bonds dictated and potentially shifted by expected movements in the markets?

a. Equity income fund
b. Growth and income fund
c. Asset allocation fund
d. Equity fund

27. Investment companies that are registered with the SEC may do all of the following EXCEPT:

a. Provide the services of a bank.
b. Sell shares with the goal of raising investment capital.
c. Loan money specifically by buying bonds or notes.
d. Borrow money under the limitation of maintaining an asset-to-debt ratio of at least 3:1.

28. All of the following statements are true of breakpoint schedules EXCEPT:

a. Investment clubs can take advantage of breakpoint sales charge reductions.
b. A mutual fund's sales charge will go down as the amount invested goes up.
c. Reductions are available to corporations.
d. Benefits the investor, the fund, and the fund's representative.

29. Open-end mutual funds have which of the following characteristics?

I. Trade in a secondary market
II. Earning potential limited only by the amount investors choose to invest
III. Offered in a continuous primary offering
IV. Fund may only repurchase shares from its own investors

a. I., II., and III.
b. II. and III.
c. II., III., and IV.
d. I. and II.

30. The mutual fund underwriting process includes all of the following EXCEPT:

a. The underwriter buys shares from the fund at the net asset value (NAV).
b. The total public offering price (POP) is equal to the net asset value (NAV) plus the underwriter's service charge.
c. The board of directors appoints the underwriter.
d. The underwriter buys shares to fill customer orders as well as to hold in inventory.

31. An investor is looking into investing in mutual fund BC. How would she calculate the public offering price (POP), given that she only knows the fund's net asset value (NAV) and sales charge percentage?

Net asset value (NAV):	$10.00
Sales charge percent:	6.5 percent

a. $10.20
b. $15.38
c. $11.55
d. $10.70

32. Which of the following are considered TRUE regarding the requirements for an investment company to be allowed to register with the SEC?

I. Investment objectives that are clearly stated and defined
II. Waiver of shareholder and net worth requirement assuming both can be satisfied within 90 days
III. Having at least 100 shareholders
IV. At least $100,000 of net worth

a. I., III., and IV.
b. I. and IV.
c. I., II., III., and IV.
d. II., III., and IV.

33. An investor has accumulated a value in his account of $59,000. His fund's breakpoint schedule states that at $75,000, he will qualify for a reduction in sales charge from his current 6.5 percent to 4 percent. If within the year the investor chooses to invest an additional $25,000 into the account, at what sales charge will that purchase be charged considering rights of accumulation?

a. 5 percent
b. 6.5 percent
c. 4 percent
d. Cannot determine, need more information

34. Determination of whether a given mutual fund is diversified involves utilizing which of the following allocation models?

a. 75-5-10 test
b. 70-5-25 test
c. 75-5-20 test
d. 80-5-5 test

35. In order for a registered representative to determine preliminary interest from clients regarding a proposed offering, she distributes a prospectus known as a "red herring." Which of the following statements accurately describes that document?

I. Name comes from the requirement for the statement on the cover to be printed in red ink, noting that the securities are not yet registered and may not be sold.
II. Usually includes a security price range.
III. All information included in this document is preliminary, including the offering price.
IV. The right to revise all information within the document is reserved.

a. I., II., and IV.
b. II., III., and IV.
c. I. and IV.
d. I., II., III., and IV.

36. For firms to become FINRA members, they must do which of the following?

a. Demonstrate that supervision of the firm is undertaken by at least two principals.
b. Provide a detailed business plan.
c. Be party to a pre-membership interview.
d. All of the above

37. Mutual fund shareholders are given voting rights by virtue of share ownership and according to the amount of shares they own. For which of these issues are they provided the right to vote?

a. Decisions regarding financial lending.
b. Decisions whether to embark on various real estate transactions.
c. Decisions regarding a change in the fund's load/no-load status.
d. All of the above

38. An investor makes a series of monthly investment deposits, each $50, over a period of five months. The total investment over that period was $250, the total number of shares that were purchased was 12, and the total of the purchase prices was $24.25. Calculate for the investor both her average cost and price per share.

a. $60, $4.85
b. $20.83, $4.85
c. $50, $2.02
d. $50, $2.83

39. The Code of Procedure:

a. Provides FINRA with a regulatory framework to govern rule violations and the investigations of complaints.
b. Provides dispute resolution between members, customers, and banks.
c. Provides guidelines for fair and equitable business between members and the public.
d. Provides guidelines for appropriate business practices between FINRA members.

40. The Uniform Gift to Minors Act was established to regulate accounts that are utilized for the benefit of a minor. Which of the following are required for ALL accounts?

a. An account title that includes the "Uniform Gift to Minors Act" and the state in which the account is registered.
b. One individual custodian.
c. Assets that will be registered in the child's name, once he is no longer a minor.
d. All of the above

41. Underwriters are required to provide an offering of all securities in a new issue to the public. They are strictly prohibited from withholding securities for which of the following groups?

a. Those financially dependent on a firm employee
b. Those working for other NASD member organizations
c. Another broker-dealer organization
d. All of the above

42. All of the following are true regarding the final prospectus distributed to purchasers of securities EXCEPT:

a. Must include pertinent information regarding substantial shareholders currently within the company.
b. Having the final prospectus available to a given client only on the SEC's website does not qualify as adequately providing it to them.
c. Serves as full and complete disclosure to potential investors regarding the securities offering.
d. Must include any known and potential risks to the purchasers of these securities.

43. In order to participate in securities transactions, it is necessary to become a registered FINRA associated person. Put the following steps in the registration process in the order in which they must occur.

I. A firm principal should sign the applicant's U-4 application verifying that she's reviewed their background.
II. The member firm must submit the applicant's U-4 application.
III. The sponsoring FINRA member firm must verify the applicant's professional résumé and character, as well as his educational record.
IV. Applicant must be fingerprinted.

a. IV., III., I., and II.
b. I., III., IV., and II.
c. III., I., IV., and II.
d. III., IV., I., and II.

44. An investor who would like to obtain a fixed and specific amount of money from his fund account on a regular basis through the fund's sale of enough shares to satisfy the specified amount would be participating in which withdrawal plan?

a. Fixed share
b. Fixed percentage
c. Fixed dollar amount
d. Fixed time

45. FINRA member fees include all of the following EXCEPT:

a. Branch office fees.
b. A fee whose size is relationally dictated by the firm's net income.
c. Representative and principal fees.
d. A basic membership fee.

46. Which of the following specifically provided the Federal Reserve Board authority over lenders?

a. Regulation G
b. Regulation U
c. Regulation T
d. All of the above

47. Which of the following can be described as offering limited information to potential investors regarding a new security issue, is utilized during the registration cooling-off period to advertise a new issue, and does not need to be filed with the SEC?

a. Red herring
b. Final prospectus
c. Tombstone ad
d. None of the above

48. The expense ratio of a mutual fund can be characterized by all of the following EXCEPT:

a. Generally, the more aggressive the fund is, the more costly it is to operate.
b. A higher ratio indicates that the fund's operational costs are higher.
c. Is a great indicator of a fund's profitability.
d. This ratio demonstrates the relationship between a fund's expenses and its average net assets.

49. In the event that a misrepresentation is found to have occurred within a securities offering prospectus, all of the following EXCEPT who can be held accountable by the purchaser for financial relief and compensation?

a. All individuals who participated in the signing of the registration statement
b. Officers and directors of the issuing organization
c. All business professionals, such as attorneys and accountants, who aided in the preparation of the registration statement
d. SEC

50. Of the following statements, which is TRUE in relation to the resignation of a registered representative?

a. Working outside of the industry for more than 24 months requires that representative to requalify by exam to reenter.
b. The member firm must submit a U-5 with FINRA within 10 days of notice.
c. Under certain conditions, a representative may transfer her registration from one firm to another.
d. There are no exceptions for military personnel regarding the 24-month inactive rule that requires requalification after working outside of the industry for that period of time or more.

51. The SEC acts as an authority within the securities industry. All of the following are true of the SEC except:

a. It's a self-regulatory organization.
b. Exchanges are required to file a registration statement with it.
c. Broker-dealers doing business with the public must register with it.
d. The president appoints five commissioners to it.

52. When opening a new account, investors are offered choices as to where they would like their securities held. Of the three options available, which one involves the securities being registered in the name of the brokerage firm and held?

a. Hold in street name
b. Transfer and hold
c. Transfer and ship
d. None of the above

53. Which of the following established the requirements for broker-dealer registration, was responsible for the creation of the SEC, and provided regulation of short sales and the secondary market?

a. The Securities Act of 1933
b. The Securities Exchange Act of 1934
c. The Maloney Act of 1938
d. FINRA rule 5130

54. Registered representatives may be terminated for all of the following EXCEPT:

a. When they have violated security laws, either federal or state.
b. When they have committed a violation of the rules of any industry regulator.
c. When they have violated firm policy.
d. When they are under investigation by an industry regulator, even given that the investigation is still ongoing.

55. Gifts into a Uniform Gifts to Minors Act account are characterized by which of the following statements?

I. May be used for the minor's education.
II. The dollar limit for the gift is set at $14,000.
III. May be cash and securities.
IV. Once given, any gift into the account is irrevocable.

a. I., III., and IV.
b. I., II., and III.
c. III. and IV.
d. III. only

56. An investor would like to calculate the cost base of his investment shares utilizing the average cost method. His investments were purchased over multiple transactions accumulated over a period of time. Calculate their cost base using the average cost method and the following information.

Total dollars invested:	$34,250
Total # of shares purchased:	475
Cost per share of last purchase transaction:	$65.45

a. $72.87
b. $71.35
c. $72.11
d. None of the above

57. Considering a discretionary account, a registered representative has the authority to do (WITHOUT prior consultation with the client) all of the following EXCEPT:

a. Decide to buy or sell.
b. Determine the amount to be bought or sold.
c. Transfer discretionary authority to a fellow representative at the firm in the event of his absence.
d. Determine the specific asset that will actually be bought or sold.

58. Which NASD bylaw governs recommendations made to customers, statements made by registered representatives, and commissions?

a. The uniform practice code
b. The code of arbitration
c. The rules of fair practice
d. The code of procedure

59. Which of the following acts as an indicator of the length of time a fund holds on to its securities?

a. Average cost
b. Portfolio turnover
c. Current yield
d. Expense ratio

60. An investor opens an account and then proceeds to purchase mutual fund shares utilizing one of three methods. One option is through a lump sum deposit, which is:

a. Utilizing a contract to invest a fixed amount over a period of time and although not contractually binding to the investor, penalties are set to be incurred upon failure to perform as the contract states.
b. Utilizing a schedule for making investment deposits on a regular basis.
c. Making a deposit of a fixed amount of money into a fund and leaving investment authority for that amount with the fund.
d. None of the above

61. The custodian of a Uniform Gifts to Minors Act (UGMA) account must manage the account on behalf of the minor within reason. All of the following are true of this management EXCEPT:

a. The custodian may not transfer authority to a third party in her absence.
b. The custodian may not borrow funds from the account.
c. There can be no utilization of margin accounts.
d. Reinvestment of any account distributions must be made within 60 days of receipt.

62. Which of the following is TRUE of the "wash sale rule"?

I. Total number of days is 60.
II. The sale date is included.
III. The investor holding period is 30 days.
IV. The number of days to be waited before repurchasing is 30.

a. II., III. and IV.
b. I. and IV.
c. II. and III.
d. I., II., and IV.

63. There are types of accounts that provide for someone other than the beneficial owner to place orders for an account. All of the following are considered that type of account EXCEPT:

a. Fiduciary account
b. Discretionary account
c. Custodial account
d. Individual account

64. When comparing front-end load plans versus spread load plans, which of the following is the primary difference between the two?

a. Maximum sales charge allowable over the life of the plan.
b. Maximum sales charge allowable in the first year.
c. Right to cancel the plan after 45 days.
d. All of the above apply to both plans.

65. The following are TRUE of new customer accounts:

I. The representative responsible for bringing the account to the firm must sign the new account card.
II. The principal of the firm must provide approval in writing of a new customer account before the first trade.
III. Within 14 days of opening the account, the firm must send the customer a copy of the new account form.
IV. A new customer who is unwilling to share his financial information will not be allowed to open an account.

a. II. and IV.
b. I., II., III., and IV.
c. I. only
d. II., III., and IV.

66. All of the following are true of mutual fund voting rights EXCEPT:

a. A vote is won with 51 percent of outstanding shares.
b. Shareholders all have the same amount of votes regardless of the amount of shares they actually have.
c. Shareholders are given the opportunity to vote on issues primary to the fund.
d. All of the above

67. Registered representatives are required to examine different investment factors when considering the appropriateness of a given mutual fund for their client and their specific investment objectives. Which of the following are included in the primary factors to be examined by the representative?

I. Services such as conversion privileges and breakpoint schedules
II. Voting rights
III. Fund performance
IV. Costs such as 12B-1 fees

a. I., III., and IV.
b. III. only
c. I. and III.
d. III. and IV.

68. A joint account involves:

a. The owner designating in advance a beneficiary to whom the assets will be transferred to upon her death.
b. Ownership by two or more adults, all having full discretion over decisions regarding the account as well as sharing equally in its benefits, and all parties being alive.
c. Upon the death of one of the owners, the assets of that owner transferring to their estate and not going to the surviving owner.
d. Upon the death of one of the owners, the surviving owner taking on the role of sole owner of the account, with all assets being transferred into her name.

69. Which of the following is described as an incentive for customers who are investing in annuities and involves an additional contribution being made to their account based on the premium they paid on the account?

a. Variable annuity
b. Combination annuity
c. Periodic payment deferred annuity
d. Bonus annuity

70. Which of the following are TRUE of a firm's efforts to prevent anti-laundering activity?

a. Firms must maintain current lists of individuals suspected to be threats to the US as obtained from the Office of Foreign Asset Control (OFAC).
b. Firms must clear all customers' identities by processing them through a list of known or suspected terrorists.
c. Upon discovering that an individual or entity is on the "threat list," a firm is required to freeze their assets and/or cease doing business with them.
d. All of the above

71. Any mutual fund advertising that may be disseminated to customers should include all of the following EXCEPT:

a. All graphs and charts should have their sources cited.
b. Fund performance for either 10 years or, if shorter, the life of the fund.
c. General information regarding the fund's sales charges.
d. None of the above

72. Which of the following activities would be considered prohibitive under the FINRA rules of fair practice?

I. A representative knowingly communicates to his customer some but not all of the transaction and firm fees the customer is to be charged.
II. A representative makes an investment recommendation to a group of his customers who have a range of risk tolerances and investment objectives. They all act on his advice and as a result all profit from that advice.
III. A representative knowingly refrains from communicating information that would be necessary to that customer making an intelligent investment decision regarding a transaction. The customer proceeds with the transaction and it is profitable to him.
IV. A representative executes on a transaction without their customer's knowledge and without the proper authorization. The trade results in a large profit to the customer.

a. I., II., III., and IV.
b. III. and IV.
c. I., III., and IV.
d. IV. only

73. Principals oversee firm activities and specifically must approve of all of the following EXCEPT:

a. All retail communications initiated by the firm.
b. All correspondence initiated by the firm.
c. All prospective employees to the firm prior to an offer of employment.
d. All new accounts to the firm.

74. Which industry violation involves a representative choosing to sell, without approval from her employing firm, products that her employer does not sell?

a. Selling away
b. Backing away
c. Sell out
d. None of the above

75. All of the following statements are true regarding representatives disclosing customer information EXCEPT:

a. A representative may NOT share or use information gained from a client relationship when the client is an issuer of securities.
b. If the client is a paying agent, there is no restriction against a representative utilizing information gained from that relationship for his benefit.
c. Customer information may not be shared with a third party without their permission.
d. None of the above

76. Which of the following provided for requirements regarding broker-dealers having written procedures for detecting suspicious activity?

a. Securities Exchange Act of 1934
b. The Patriot Act
c. The Telephone Consumer Protection Act of 1991
d. Securities Act of 1933

77. The Telephone Consumer Protection Act of 1991 allows for the following exemption(s):

a. Any calls made to debtors of the firm who may be delinquent.
b. Any calls that the firm may make to current customers.
c. Any calls made by either a nonprofit organization or religious group.
d. All of the above

78. Which annuity payout option is described as providing the investor with contract payments for her entire life?

a. Joint with last survivor
b. Life with period certain
c. Life only/straight life
d. None of the above

79. In their attempt to prevent money laundering, member firms must:

a. Within 15 days of receiving currency, submit Form 4789 to the IRS.
b. Submit a report of currency for receipts of $10,000 or more.
c. Records of international wire transfers of $3,000 or more must be maintained.
d. All of the above

80. Which of the following are TRUE regarding representatives and the recommendations they make to their customers?

I. Representatives are free to draw any product comparisons in an effort to provide suitable recommendations for their customers.
II. Recommendations made must align with the customer's investment objectives and risk tolerance.
III. Promises of future profits may be made if they are well substantiated and backed by reliable facts.
IV. When providing recommendations, the representative must emphasize that these statements are opinion based and not factual.

a. II. only
b. II. and IV.
c. I. and II.
d. I., II., and IV.

81. Regulation S-P establishes all of the following requirements regarding the privacy of firm customers EXCEPT:

a. Every year customers should receive additional privacy notices from the firm.
b. If elected by the customer, the firm may not share his nonpublic personal information with outside businesses.
c. Customers must receive their first privacy notice from the firm within 30 days of their account being opened.
d. All of the above

82. Calculate the current yield of mutual fund MN given the information below.

MN fund annual dividends =	$4.50
MN public offering price (POP) =	$22
MN capital gains distributions =	$1.75

a. 28.41 percent
b. 7.95 percent
c. 20.45 percent
d. None of the above

83. Which of the following statements is TRUE regarding the "gift rule"?

I. The value of the gift cannot exceed $50.
II. It is permissible under certain circumstances for a broker-dealer to give a gift to another broker-dealer's employee.
III. The restriction on the gift is based on gifts per person per year only, not the dollar value of the gifts.
IV. The gift must go through the firm first and then is passed from there to the employee.

a. I. and II.
b. I., II., and IV.
c. II. and IV.
d. II. and III.

84. Under FINRA's rules of fair practice, forgery is considered to be:

a. A manipulative practice
b. A fraudulent act
c. Churning
d. A deceptive practice

85. A fixed annuity is one of the three basic types of annuities available to investors. Which of the following are characteristics of that type of investment instrument?

I. Insulated from the risk of inflation.
II. Representatives need to obtain an insurance and securities license to sell these.
III. The return is guaranteed at a specific set minimum.
IV. The portfolio consists of investments that include real estate and mortgages.

a. IV. only
b. III. and IV.
c. II. and III.
d. I., II., and IV.

86. Which regulation was established as a result of 9/11 and the business impact that occurred as a result?

a. Limited trading authorization
b. Business continuity plan
c. Prudent man rule
d. None of the above

87. In establishing an account for a non-US customer, firms must obtain certain validating documents. At least one of which of the following could that be?

I. Proof of employment
II. US tax ID number
III. Passport number, including the country that issued it
IV. Personal reference

a. I., II., and III.
b. II. and III.
c. III. and IV.
d. I. and III.

88. A registered representative who receives a minor rule violation (MRV) letter can expect which of the following?

a. Upon receipt of the letter, he will be given 10 days to accept the offer provided.
b. He will face at most a maximum penalty of a $1,500 fine.
c. Signing the letter does not eliminate his right to appeal the outcome of the procedure.
d. Signing the letter will also provide him the opportunity to admit or deny his participation in the alleged violations.

89. Two parties in dispute seek to resolve their issues in a formal manner, without personal contact and without a hearing. The disputed amount between the parties totals $36,000. Which type of resolution process would be most appropriate for these parties?

a. Simplified arbitration
b. Arbitration by panel
c. Mediation
d. None of the above

90. A representative has a customer with a very conservative investment outlook who is more concerned with the retention of her money and less interested in taking on a lot of risk to achieve large financial results. Which of the following investments should the representative discourage her from pursuing?

a. Municipal bonds
b. Government bonds
c. Common stock funds
d. High quality, high-grade corporate bonds

91. A registered representative is handed a guilty decision from the Division of Enforcement (DOE) and would like to do everything possible to continue to fight the allegations and verdict. Which of the following is NOT true of the avenues his case can take?

a. The National Adjudicatory Counsel's (NAC) verdict can be appealed to the SEC if desired.
b. If warranted, the final place of appeal will be the court system.
c. The DOE's decision may be appealed within 10 days to the NAC.
d. If the NAC finds merit to the appeal, it is required to review the case within 45 days.

92. A customer makes a formal complaint regarding a FINRA violation involving her representative. She submits the complaint to the member firm that employs her representative. From that point, who will determine whether the complaint has enough merit to initiate a formal investigation of the allegations against the representative?

a. The representative's immediate superior
b. FINRA
c. The member firm
d. All of the above through a brief summary investigation

93. A father who acts as the legal custodian of his son's Uniform Gifts to Minors Act (UGMA) account would like to transact in the account. Which of the following transactions does he have the authority to participate in as the custodian and given the restrictions on him per the UGMA?

I. A loan via margin account
II. A loan from the account of less than $750
III. Option contracts
IV. Penny stock purchase

a. III. and IV.
b. II. and III.
c. I. and III. only
d. None of the above

94. A customer is granted a monetary award as a result of the resolution of a dispute with his representative. Which of the following statements are TRUE in relation to the likelihood of receiving his awarded restitution?

a. His representative having been ordered to pay has 60 days to do so.
b. Awards are always available for appeal by either party.
c. His representative may be more motivated to pay the award, in that the penalty for non-payment is his suspension.
d. None of the above

95. A registered representative rejected the minor rule violation (MRV) offer and is proceeding with the formal hearing process to resolve the allegation complaints against him. Which of the following are possibilities for penalties he may face if found guilty of wrongdoing?

I. Maximum 18-month suspension
II. Barred for life
III. Maximum 7 year expulsion
IV. Maximum fine of $7,500

a. I., II., and III.
b. II. only
c. II. and III.
d. II., III., and IV.

96. A representative has a few different clients with a full spectrum of liquidity needs. Place the following investments in order of least liquid to most so as provide a range of investment possibilities for each of the representative's investors.

I. CMOs
II. Mutual funds
III. Real estate
IV. Annuities

a. III., I., IV., and II.
b. I., IV., II., and III.
c. II., III., I., and IV.
d. IV., III., II., and I.

97. A registered representative has just received notification that she is being investigated for an alleged FINRA violation. Which of the following is considered a possible outcome for her violation investigation?

a. FINRA may proceed with a formal hearing process.
b. FINRA could resolve the allegations through a summary complaint procedure.
c. Her case could be dismissed if after an investigation the allegations are found to be baseless.
d. All of the above

98. Corporation PX announced that it will pay a dividend of $.75 per share to all those who are shareholders of its company stock as of Monday, March 12. The ex-dividend date will be Thursday, March 8. The price per share of PX stock at close on Wednesday, March 7, was $53.95. What will be the PX price per share at the opening of the market on Thursday, March 8?

a. $53.25
b. $53.95
c. $53.10
d. $53.20

99. An investor would like to submit to his representative the information needed to be provided with the best investment recommendations possible. Which of the following topics would NOT be important in doing that?

a. His current tax bracket.
b. His current profession and future career objectives.
c. His current financial position including accurate debt loads.
d. His overall outlook regarding investing and his ability to reach His investment objectives.

100. A dispute occurs between a customer and her representative. The representative is bound to resolve it through arbitration, but needs to determine whether this particular customer has satisfied the requirements necessary to proceed with the arbitration process. Which of the following must be TRUE in order to ensure that the customer has officially agreed in advance to this type of dispute resolution, and to determine whether the dispute itself is eligible for the arbitration process?

I. The customer's receipt of a confirmation in writing that she originally agreed to arbitration as the dispute resolution option of choice.
II. The timing for arbitration being within six years of the disputed event.
III. The customer signing an agreement in advance agreeing to arbitration as the dispute resolution option of choice.
IV. The customer having been notified in advance of any restrictions there may be on the disputes that are ineligible for the arbitration process.

a. I., II., and III.
b. I. and II.
c. I., II., III., and IV.
d. III. and IV.

Answers and Explanations

1. C: The investor needs an investment grade bond that pays a high coupon. Option A is incorrect as the coupon is paid based on the face value of the bond not the market price of 1010. Option B is incorrect since CC is below investment grade and is considered speculative. Option D is incorrect since the bond is trading at a high premium of 1040 and the coupon payment is incorrect. Option C makes the most sense since the T-Bonds are only trading at a 1% premium and T-Bonds are very safe even if bought from the secondary market. The 5% coupon of a T-Bond is paid semi-annually based on the par value hence $25 each payment is correct.

2. B: The order of dates for a mutual fund's dividend distribution are the declaration date, record date, ex-dividend date, and payment date. This is different from the order of dates for common stock, which has the ex-dividend date occurring the day of or the day before the record date.

3. D: A letter of intent can be backdated for up to the previous 90 days, and will provide that if the investor fails the letter of intent, the sales charge is simply adjusted accordingly. The investor, however, has up to 13 months, not 12, to meet the level of investment committed to in the letter of intent. Additionally, the investor is not contractually bound to purchase the indicated number of shares.

4. C: The maximum amount for a sales charge that an open-end fund can charge is 8.5 percent of the public offering price (POP).

5. A: The investor will redeem fund EF shares at $9.50 and purchase fund DC shares at $19.10. Conversion privilege exchange requirements dictate that the redemption and purchase must be at the net asset value (NAV).

6. D: Money market funds will invest in debt securities with maturities of less than one year, commercial paper, and banker's acceptances.

7. A:

$$\text{assets} - \text{liabilities} = \text{Net Asset Value (NAV)}$$

$$\frac{\text{total NAV}}{\text{total \# of shares}} = \text{NAV per share}$$

$$\$25{,}000{,}000 - \$2{,}200{,}000 = \$22{,}800{,}000 \quad \text{NAV}$$

$$\frac{\$22{,}800{,}000}{4{,}500{,}000} = \$5.07 \quad \text{NAV per share}$$

8. B: The primary difference between rights of accumulation and a letter of intent is that the latter places a 13-month time limit on qualifying for the reduction where the former has NO time limit. However, for both, the reduction does not apply to previous investment purchases, qualification can be accomplished using previous investments, and current investments also go into determining sales charge reduction qualification status.

9. D: All of these methods can be utilized by an investor who wants to determine the cost base of investments that were the result of multiple purchase transactions. Share identification involves the investor keeping a record of the prices and dates of their purchases so as to utilize that information in deciding which shares will produce the most favorable results when sold. First in, first out involves the IRS taking the first shares purchased as the first to be sold, when not specifically told by the investor when selling. Average cost involves utilizing a formula to determine the average cost of all shares.

10. A: A mutual fund's prospectus should be disposed of after 16 months. The fund SHOULD update the prospectus information every 12 months, but is REQUIRED to update the information every 13 months. The fund prospectus can be utilized by the fund for up to 16 months.

11. B: $\$14 - \$17 = (\$3)$

This investor has incurred a $3 capital LOSS per share.

$$(\$3) \times 2{,}500 = (\$7{,}500)$$

Given 2,500 shares, this investor has incurred a TOTAL capital loss of $7,500.

12. C: dividend income + interest income + capital gains − expenses = net investment income

Average net assets are NOT used in the calculation of net investment income for a mutual fund.

13. A:

$$\text{investment to be made} \times \text{sales charge \%} = \text{front} - \text{end load sales charge}$$

$$\$25{,}000 \times .065 = \$1{,}625$$

14. A: The $27,000 investment purchase will be charged at the reduced 7 percent rate due to combination privileges that allow for purchases into two portfolios, done at the same time, to qualify for the applicable sales charge as a lump-sum investment instead of two separate purchases.

15. D: An investment company's registration is complete upon the SEC's receipt of its notice of registration and must include biographical info on officers and directors, any investment concentration to be focused on, and its future plans for borrowing.

16. D: For the reinvestment of each distribution there may be a service charge; if allowed to reinvest both capital gains and dividend distributions, it will be at either the NAV or at a discount to the POP; and finally, all distributions are taxed, whether they're reinvested or not.

17. B: A no-load mutual fund does not charge a sales charge and accordingly can then sell its shares directly to investors at the NAV without the aid of an underwriter. The selling group involves a brokerage firm buying shares at a discount from the public offering price (POP) based on a previously established selling agreement and then going on to sell them to investors at the POP. An underwriter buys shares from the fund at the net asset value (NAV), charges a service charge for its services, and then sells the shares to investors at the public offering price (POP), the NAV plus service charge.

18. D: All of the statements are TRUE given that the investor's conversion transaction is done at the share's NAV, the sales charge is waived if done within 30 days, and no commissions are paid.

19. B: Securities being purchased and sold within the portfolio will NOT have a changing impact on the mutual fund's NAV. When the portfolio manager of a mutual fund purchases securities, the value of the securities in the fund goes up at the same rate as the amount of cash used to purchase the securities in the fund goes down. However, dividend distributions, security prices rising and falling, and bond interest payments WILL change the fund's NAV.

20. B: Money market funds must carry one of the top two ratings from the industry-recognized rating agencies, and the securities must NOT have maturities exceeding 13 months. However, the portfolio securities must have an average maturity of no more than 90 days, not 180, and the assets must not exceed 5 percent of a single issuer's securities, not 8 percent.

21. B: A back-end load charge can also be referred to as a contingent deferred sales charge (CDSC). A level load sales charge is based on the NAV, and an asset-based fee is charged quarterly.

22. B: Unit investment trusts (UITs) are investments in either a fixed or non-fixed portfolio, are not actively managed, and offer shares as a representation of investment interest. A face-amount company has an investor contracting to deposit monies in a lump sum or installments so as to receive a fixed amount of money at some specific date in the future. Real estate investment trusts are not considered to be an investment company under the Act. Management investment companies may be open or closed-end and are actively managed by an adviser.

23. C: $\frac{\text{Public Offering Price (POP)} - \text{Net Asset Value (NAV)}}{\text{Public Offering Price}} = \text{sales charge \%}$

$$\frac{(8.50 - 8.00)}{8.50} = 0.0588 = 5.9\%$$

24. D: Government bond fund dividends ARE taxed federally. Bond funds can be municipal, government, and corporate. The investment made is in a portfolio of debt, and investor income is mainly the result of interest payments.

25. C: A statement of additional information will include information such as the balance sheet and income statement. The advertising prospectus is the summary prospectus with additional information regarding past performance, and the most common prospectus given to the majority of investors is known as the summary prospectus.

26. C: Asset allocation funds make investment decisions based on the fund manager's expectations for movements in the market. Equity income funds have as their main focus investments that pay consistent dividends. Growth and income funds focus on both capital appreciation and income resulting from dividend payments. Equity funds primarily seek capital appreciation.

27. A: Registered investment companies CANNOT provide services that a bank or savings and loan would. They CAN, however, sell shares, loan money by buying bonds, and borrow money while maintaining a 3:1 asset-to-debt ratio.

28. A: Breakpoint sales charge reductions are NOT available to investment clubs. They can be described as the process by which the sales charge decreases according to a rise in the investment made. The reductions in sales charge ARE available to corporations and these reductions benefit the investor, fund, and the fund's rep.

29. C: Open-end mutual funds have earning potential that is limited only by the amount of funds investors choose to contribute, are offered in a continuous primary offering, and have shares that can only be repurchased from its own investors. Only closed-end funds trade in a secondary market.

30. D: Underwriters only purchase shares with the intent to fill current orders and may not purchase shares to be held in inventory. Underwriters do buy shares at the NAV. The POP is the NAV plus the underwriter's service charge, and the board of directors is responsible for appointing the fund's underwriter.

31. D: $\frac{\text{Net Asset Value (NAV)}}{(100\%-\text{sales charge }\%)} = \text{Public Offering Price (POP)}$

$$\frac{10.00}{(100\% - 6.5\%)} = \frac{10}{93.5\%} = \frac{10}{.935} = \$10.70$$

32. C: The three main requirements for being allowed to register with the SEC are defined investment objectives, at least 100 shareholders, and a net worth of at least $100,000; however, the last two requirements may be waived preliminarily as long as both will be fulfilled within 90 days.

33. C: The sales charge he will be charged for the last investment purchase of $25,000 will be at the reduced 4 percent. Considering rights of accumulation, once the investor reaches the investment point that qualifies for the next reduction in sales charge (as referenced by the fund's breakpoint schedule), the reduced rate will apply to current and future investment purchases.

34. A: The Investment Company Act of 1940 established an allocation model known as the 75-5-10 test that is used to determine whether a mutual fund is diversified by requiring it to have 75 percent of assets from outside issuers, a 5 percent limit on investing in any one company, and a 10 percent maximum on ownership of a company's overall outstanding voting stock.

35. A: A red herring preliminary prospectus has its name originating from the red inked statement required to be printed on the cover, usually includes a price range for the security, and can have any and all of its information revised prior to the final prospectus.

36. D: In order for firms to become FINRA members, they must show that the firm is being supervised by at least two principals, provide a detailed business plan, and have a pre-membership interview.

37. D: Mutual fund shareholders are allowed voting rights regarding financial lending, real estate transactions, and the fund's load/no-load status.

38. B: $\frac{\text{total of dollars they invested}}{\text{total shares they purchased}} = \text{average cost}$

$$\frac{\text{total of their purchase prices}}{\text{number of purchases made}} = \text{average price}$$

$$\frac{\$250}{12} = \$20.83 \quad \text{average cost}$$

$$\frac{\$24.25}{5} = \$4.85 \quad \text{average price}$$

39. A: The Code of Procedure provides a regulatory framework related to violations and complaints. Dispute resolution comes from the Code of Arbitration, the Rules of Fair Practice provide guidelines regarding fair business between members and the public, and the Uniform Practice Code guides appropriate business practices between FINRA members.

40. D: All UGMA accounts must have, among other requirements, the UGMA and state of the account in the title, one single custodian, and assets that will be registered to the child once he or she is no longer a minor.

41. D: Underwriters are prohibited from withholding securities for financial dependents of firm employees, employees of other NASD member organizations, and other broker-dealers.

42. B: The final prospectus being provided for viewing on the SEC's website WILL qualify as satisfying the "access equals delivery" rule and, accordingly, having been adequately and universally provided to potential investors. It must also include information regarding current substantial shareholders of the company, and any known risks to investors in the securities. It also serves as full disclosure of the offering to potential investors.

43. C: The registration process steps start with the firm investigating and verifying the applicant's background information and then signing his U-4 application certifying its review. Next the applicant is fingerprinted so as to then have the member firm submit his U-4 application.

44. C: An investor requesting a fixed amount on a regular basis through the sale of just enough shares to satisfy the amount is participating in the fixed-dollar amount. The fixed-share plan calls for the investor to designate a fixed number of shares to be sold on a regular basis so as to collect the proceeds. The fixed-percentage plan calls for the fund to redeem a certain percentage of an investor's account as designated by him with the proceeds then forwarded to him. A fixed-time plan calls for an investor to designate to have the value of her account divided equally and paid out to her over a specified period of time.

45. B: There is no FINRA member fee based on a firm's net income, but there IS one based on a firm's gross income. Other FINRA membership fees include those for branch offices, representatives and principals, and a basic fee.

46. D: Regulations G, U, and T all provide the Federal Reserve authority over the lending activities of commercial lenders, banks, and broker-dealers respectively.

47. C: A tombstone ad aids in advertising during the registration cooling-off period, and does not need to be filed with the SEC. A red herring is a preliminary prospectus utilized in determining client interest and contains a majority of the information that the final prospectus will contain. The final prospectus offers full disclosure to purchasers of the securities and will be filed with the SEC.

48. C: A mutual fund's expense ratio is NOT a great indicator of a fund's profitability, but instead indicates a fund's operational efficiency. A higher ratio does indicate higher operational costs, the ratio shows the relationship between a fund's expenses and assets, and generally it helps in demonstrating that the more aggressive the fund is, the higher the operational costs will be.

49. D: The SEC may NOT be held accountable by investors seeking financial relief as a result of a misrepresentation occurring with an offering prospectus. The SEC has the role of reviewing the offering registration statement and prospectus, but does NOT guarantee accuracies or provide approval of the securities. Financial retribution can be sought from all individuals who signed the registration statement, officers and directors of the organization, and attorneys and accountants who helped prepare the registration statement.

50. A: If a registered representative resigns and works away from the industry for 24 or more months, he must then requalify by exam if he would like to reenter and work within it again. The member firm must file the U-5 with FINRA within 30 days, not 10. Under NO circumstances is a representative's registration transferable from one firm to another. Military personnel are excused from abiding by the rule that requires reexamination after being away from the industry for 24 or more months.

51. A: The SEC is NOT a self-regulatory organization. It IS, however, the organization that exchanges and broker-dealers must register with, and operates with five commissioners who are appointed by the president.

52. A: "Hold in street name" is the method that allows for the securities to be registered in the name of the brokerage firm so as to simplify the transfer of ownership; the securities are then held by the firm. "Transfer and hold" is the method where the securities are registered in the name of the customer and then held by the firm. "Transfer and ship" is the method where the securities are registered in the name of customers and then shipped to the address of their choice.

53. B: The Securities Exchange Act of 1934 established broker-dealer registration requirements, created the SEC, provided short-sale regulations, and currently acts to regulate the secondary market. The Securities Act of 1933 provides regulation of the primary market. The Maloney Act of 1938 is responsible for the creation of the National Association of Securities Dealers (NASD).

54. D: Registered representatives may NOT be terminated if under investigation and that investigation is still ongoing. They MAY be terminated for violating security laws, industry regulator rules, or a firm policy.

55. A: Gifts into a UGMA account have NO dollar limit. The gifts may be used for the minor's education, may be cash or securities, and once given are irrevocable.

56. C: $\frac{\text{total dollars invested}}{\text{total \# of shares purchased}} = \text{average cost}$

$$\frac{\$34{,}250}{475} = \$72.11$$

57. C: A registered representative with discretionary authority CANNOT transfer discretionary authority to anyone inside or outside the firm. They CAN, however, make the decision to buy or sell, determine the amount to buy or sell, and decide the specific asset to buy or sell.

58. C: The rules of fair practice govern customer recommendations, statements made by representatives, and commissions. The uniform practice code establishes how FINRA members transact business among themselves. The code of arbitration is for dispute resolution, and the code of procedure establishes regulations for how FINRA handles violations.

59. B: A fund's portfolio turnover will act as an indicator of the length of time it held on to its securities. Average cost is a method of calculating cost base, current yield indicates the level of income produced for every dollar invested, and expense ratio is an indicator of a fund's operational efficiency.

60. C: The lump sum method involves depositing a fixed amount of money and leaving decision-making authority over that money with the fund. Utilizing a contract to invest a fixed amount with penalties incurred if not completed is a contractual accumulation plan. Utilizing a schedule for making regular deposits into the fund is a voluntary accumulation plan.

61. D: Reinvestment of any account distributions are not held to a specific period of time, but need only be reinvested within a "reasonable time" from receipt. The custodian must not transfer authority to another party, borrow funds from the account, or utilize margin accounts.

62. A: The "wash sale rule" states that the days to be included are the investor's sale date (1 day), and then the holding period (30 days) and waiting period (30 days) the investor must wait before repurchasing the securities, or something very similar. The total number of days therefore is 61.

63. D: An individual account is simply that owned by one person, with the authority to make all decisions and place all orders singularly held by that individual. A fiduciary account provides for a trustee to be given authority to place orders, a discretionary account provides for a registered representative to have limited power over the account, and a custodial account provides for a custodian to be given authority over the account on behalf of minor/owner.

64. B: The maximum sales charge allowable in the first year is the primary difference, with the front-end load being 50 percent and the spread load being 20 percent. Both plans have a maximum sales charge over the life of the plan of 9 percent, and a right to cancel after 45 days.

65. C: The representative who initiated the new account in the firm must sign the new account card. The principal of the firm must provide approval of the new account EITHER before or right after the first trade. The firm must send the new customer a copy of the new account form within 30 days of the account opening, and a new customer who is unwilling to share his financial information CAN still open an account, assuming he can provide proof of his ability to transact within the account.

66. B: Voting rights for mutual fund shareholders are determined by the amount of shares, not simply based on their being shareholders. The more shares you have, the more votes that follow. Further, a vote is won by a simple majority of 51 percent, and shareholders vote on primary fund issues.

67. A: The primary factors to be examined by the representative before recommending a mutual fund as an investment for her client include services, performance, and costs. Voting rights are not considered to be a major issue the representative is obligated to examine prior to making an investment recommendation to her client.

68. B: A joint account is two or more adults, both needing be alive and sharing equally in discretion and benefits of the account. Transfer on death is the account where the owner designates in advance a beneficiary for the account in the event of his or her death. Joint tenants in common is an account where upon the death of one of the owners their assets are transferred into their estate and do not go to the surviving owner. Joint tenants with rights to survivorship has the surviving owner becoming the sole owner of the account in the event of the other owner's death.

69. D: A bonus annuity, specifically a premium enhancement, is an incentive in the form of an additional contribution to an annuity investor's account, and its size is based on the premium they paid. A variable annuity offers a higher rate of return and no guaranteed rate of return. A combination annuity has both a fixed and variable portion. A periodic payment deferred annuity allows for the investor to make scheduled payments and has more flexible terms.

70. D: In an effort to prevent, detect, and manage the effects of anti-laundering activity, firms must stay current of "threat lists" obtained through the Office of Foreign Asset Control (OFAC), clear all customers versus a list of known or suspected terrorists, and freeze the assets or cease doing business with anyone appearing on the "threat list."

71. C: Mutual fund advertising should go beyond general information regarding the fund's sales charges, and instead state specifically the highest sales charge that may be charged by the fund. Additionally, all charts and graphs should have their sources cited, and fund performance for either the last 10 years of the fund or, if shorter, the life of the fund, should be provided.

72. A: All of these scenarios would be prohibitive under the FINRA rules of fair practice. Representatives must present ALL fees to their customers clearly and without misrepresentation or omission. It is considered bad conduct for a representative to provide "blanket recommendations" to a group of investors regardless of whether the outcome results in profit to the investors or not. Omitting material facts regarding an investment decision is prohibited even if the facts were positive in nature and the end result of the transaction was profitable to the customer. Unauthorized trading on a customer's account is against FINRA rules whether the resulting transaction produces profit for the customer or not.

73. C: Principals of a firm do NOT need to approve all prospective employees prior to them being offered employment. They must, however, approve all retail communications, correspondence, and new accounts.

74. A: Selling away occurs when representatives sell products their firm does not and, further, do it without disclosing it to them. Backing away occurs when an over-the-counter market maker does not honor its firm quotes. A sell out is the broker-dealer's transaction that occurs as a result of a customer not providing payment to it for securities purchased.

75. B: Representatives may NOT utilize for their own benefit information gained from a client relationship with a paying agent or a securities issuer. Customer information cannot be shared with a third party without the permission of that customer.

76. B: The Patriot Act provided requirements for broker-dealers to take actions to detect suspicious activity. The Securities Exchange Act of 1934 is responsible for the creation of the SEC. The Telephone Consumer Protection Act of 1991 provides regulations regarding the calling of prospective customers at home. The Securities Act of 1933 establishes rules to govern the primary market.

77. D: Exempt from the Telephone Consumer Protection Act of 1991 are calls made to debtors who are delinquent, current customers, and calls made from a nonprofit organization or religious group.

78. C: Life only/straight life provides the investor with contract payments for his entire life, ending at the time of his death. Joint with last survivor provides the opportunity for the annuity to be owned jointly by more than one investor, with payments coming to an end upon the death of the final surviving contract owner. Life with period certain pays on the contract to the investor, to his beneficiaries upon the death of the investor, OR pays for a specific period of time selected in advance by the investor. Whichever of these options is longer will dictate the length of time payments will continue.

79. D: To prevent money laundering, firms must notify the IRS within 15 days of receiving currency, submit currency reports for $10,000 or more, and maintain records for international wire transfers of $3,000 or more.

80. B: A representative's recommendations must align with her customer's investment objectives and risk tolerance, and when providing those recommendations, she must clearly communicate that any statements made are opinion based, and not fact. Representatives may NOT make comparisons of products that are dissimilar or result in confusion for the customer, or make promises of future profits, regardless of whether they're substantiated by fact or not.

81. C: Regulation S-P requires the firm to send a customer his first privacy notice no later than the opening of his account, NOT within 30 days. Additionally, it must send its customers privacy notices annually, and if the customer has elected against it, it is prohibited from sharing the customer's personal information with outside businesses.

82. C: $\frac{\text{fund annual income}}{\text{current price}} = \text{current yield}$

$$\frac{\$4.50}{\$22} = .2045 = 20.45\%$$

83. C: The gift rule states that it is permissible for a broker-dealer to provide a gift to the employee of another broker-dealer, given the limitation that the gift has a value of less than $100 per person per year, and the gift must be given to the firm to then be passed along to the recipient employee.

84. B: Under FINRA's rules of fair practice, forgery is considered to be a fraudulent act and is strictly prohibited. A manipulative or deceptive practice is one that individuals engage in so as to gain an unfair advantage over another individual. Churning involves a representative participating in an excessive number of transactions in an effort to accumulate higher commissions.

85. B: Fixed annuities have a return that is guaranteed at a specific set minimum and a portfolio of investments that include real estate and mortgages. They ARE susceptible to the risk of inflation and representatives need to ONLY obtain an insurance license to be allowed to market and sell these instruments to customers.

86. B: The regulation that was established due to the business aftermath of 9/11 was the business continuity plan. A limited trading authorization involves a customer giving permission to a representative or firm to trade on her account without getting her approval beforehand. The prudent man rule regulates fiduciaries and the investment decisions they make on behalf of third parties.

87. B: Establishing an account for a non-US customer requires that the firm obtain at least one of the following: US tax ID number, passport number and country of issuance, alien ID number, or information from another government-issued ID. Proof of employment and a personal reference are NOT options for validating documents to be obtained by the broker-dealer in establishing an account.

88. A: Upon receiving a minor rule violation letter, this representative can expect to have 10 days to respond to the offer outlined in the letter. He can expect to face a penalty involving a censure and maximum $2,500 fine, NOT $1,500. By signing the letter, he IS giving up his right to appeal the outcome of the MRV procedure, and he is NOT admitting or denying his participation in the alleged violating activities.

89. A: Simplified arbitration is suitable for disputes involving amounts less than $50,000 and substitutes the opportunity for a hearing with a submission in writing by both parties. An arbitration by panel involves a hearing with up to three arbitrators. Mediation is an informal process necessitating a meeting of the two parties to resolve the issues at hand.

90. C: With a customer who is seeking more conservative investments and less risky reinvestment of gains, one of the investments she should avoid are common stock funds. Investment choices that would be appropriate for her would be municipal bonds, government bonds, and high-grade corporate bonds.

91. C: The representative, if he chooses to, must appeal the DOE's decision to the NAC within 15 days, NOT 10. If finding merit in the appeal, the NAC must review the case within 45 days. The NAC's verdict can be appealed with the SEC, and further, the court system if necessary.

92. B: Given a customer complaint of a registered representative involving a FINRA violation, only FINRA can determine whether the allegations have the merit necessary to launch a formal investigation of the representative. The representative's immediate superior and his member firm will only act to elevate the allegations to FINRA for review and will not determine merit.

93. D: This father as custodian of his son's account may NOT acquire a loan via margin account OR from the account itself, regardless of the amount. Further, he may NOT transact in options or penny stock purchases.

94. C: It is true that the representative may be more motivated to pay the award in order to avoid suspension. The representative actually must pay within 30 days, NOT 60. The award the representative was ordered to pay is NOT available for appeal.

95. B: If found guilty of the allegations against him, one of the penalties that may be imposed against him is that he may be barred for life from the organization. Additionally, he might face a maximum suspension of up to 12 months (NOT 18 months), a maximum expulsion of up to 10 years (NOT 7 years), and a fine of ANY amount.

96. A: The investment choices from least liquid to most are real estate, CMOs, annuities, and mutual funds.

97. D: The registered representative being investigated can expect her case to be resolved through a formal hearing process, a summary complaint procedure, or if found to be having no merit, could be dismissed.

98. D: Prior to the ex-dividend date, stock PX will trade with the value of the declared dividend included in the price. On and after the ex-dividend date, stock PX will trade without the value of the dividend included, and shareholders purchasing after that date will not receive the dividend. Because of that, on and after the ex-dividend date, the price per share will be the prior day's close minus the dividend amount that was paid out.

Here, it would be:

$$\$53.95 - \$.75 = \$53.20$$

99. B: In order to enable her representative to provide her with the best investment recommendations, the customer should be prepared to discuss with the representative her tax bracket, financial position, and investment outlook. It is NOT necessary for her, in seeking appropriate investment recommendations, to discuss her profession or future career objectives.

100. C: In order for this customer to be bound to proceeding with arbitration for this particular dispute, he must have signed an agreement accepting arbitration as his dispute resolution choice and have received written receipt of his agreement to do so. He must have also been notified of the specific disputes that are ineligible for arbitration. Finally, the dispute must have originated within six years of the proposed initiation of the arbitration process.

It's Your Moment, Let's Celebrate It!

Share your story @mometrixtestpreparation